Princess Anne County
Virginia
List of Earmarks and Brands
1691 – 1778

Transcribed by Michael Schoettle

Printed in the United States of America

Privately published by Michael Schoettle

Published 2015 by
Michael Schoettle
17041 Thousand Oaks Dr
Haymarket, VA 20169

This book and others may be purchased by contacting the author directly.

Introduction

This work was transcribed from Microfilm Reel Number 38 at the Library of Virginia. These records were in a separate section in front of Order Book 1.

The page numbers referenced in the index are the pages to this book, not the original pages.

There are many other ear marks noted in the Princess Anne County Deed Books and Order Books. These marks are not included in this transcription but will be part of my transcriptions of these books that will eventually be published.

Spelling errors were purposefully included. Such as slitt, sloop, etc

The list was not in chronological order. The original order of the pages were two loose sheets then Pages a thru t followed by Pages 1 thru 20.

> Two loose sheets of paper from May 1696 and Jun 1712.
>
> Pages a – s covered the date range of Dec 1753 thru Sep 1778.
>
> Page t covered Jan 1753 thru Jun 1753. There is one entry at the top of Page t that has no date. My best guess would be this entry is from June 1752 and that page t is chronologically before page a.
>
> Page 1 – 20 covered 1691 thru Nov 1751. The bottom of page 20 has several entries from 1761.

As always, I strongly recommend to verify the information with the original source document.

1753	
December	Charles Gasking his mark is crop & slit the left ear the right whole
	Doct[r] George Roueriers his mark is crop the left ear over keel & slit the right ear
	James Moores mark is crop & two slits either ear & crop & under keel the contrary
1754 Jany	Robert Huggins his mark is slit the right ear & under half crop the left ear
	John Harper Jun his mark is swallow fork each ear
	Jonathan Bonney his mark is crop & nick under both ears
	Richard Bonney his mark is crop & under half crop the right ear crop & slit the left
	Jonathan Buskey his mark is swallow fork the right ear crop under & over keel the left ear
	Maximilian Boush Junr his mark is crop & hole either ear & crop the contrary
	John Stone Jun[r] his mark is swallow fork & under keel the left & over keel the right
	Salle Stone her mark is swallow fork & under keel the right ear & slit the left
	Lewis Baker his mark is slit the (blank) ear swallow fork & ____ the (blank)
	William Whitehard his mark is slit the right ear swallow fork & under half the left ear
	William Pooles mark is swallow fork the right ear flower deluce & slit the left ear
	Anthony Whitehurst's mark is swallow fork and under keel the right ear & slit out the left
	William / son of Jeremiah Henley his mark is crop hole & under keel the right ear & over keel the left ear
	Lemuel Newton his mark is under one tooth the right ear crop & two slits the left ear
	William Short his mark is slit out either ear the other ear whole
	Adam Robertsons mark is slit & under keel the right ear & under keel the left ear
	Francis Sayer his mark is slit & nick under the right & under keel the left
	Sarah Bannister her mark is crop & three slits the right ear & a hole in the left ear
	Purin Smyths mark is crop & slit the right ear & over one tooth the left ear
	Solomon Wilkins his mark is under half crop & nick under the right ear & under half crop the left ear
	John Creeds mark is crop & under half crop the right ear, swallow fork and under keel the left ear
	John Cason his mark is crop & under half crop the right ear swallow fork the left ear
	James / son of said John / Cason his mark is crop & under half crop the right ear swallow fork & flower deluce the left ear

Laughlin M^c^cabe his mark is swallow fork & over keel the right ear slit and under keel the left ear which mark belonged to Pat Murphy & given by him to the said M^c^cabe

Anthony Barns Junr his mark is under half crop either ear & under keel & slit the contrary ear

William Brinson his mark is crop over keel & a hole the right ear & crop & over keel the left

Jonathan Jackson his mark is under keel & slit both ears

Page b

1754

Sept 12 John Bonney / son of William / his mark is crop & nick under the right ear & over keel the left ear

Idems mark also is crop & nick under the right ear & crop & over keel the left ear

William Shepards mark is under keel the right ear & swallow fork the left

John Williamson Sen his mark is a nick under the right ear and swallow fork the left ear

William Haynes his mark is crop slit & over half crop the right ear cop & under half crop the left ear

John Willis his mark is nick under the right ear crop & three slits the left ear

1755 Thos Haynes his mark is swallow fork under & over keel the right & left ears

William Davis his mark is over keel the right ear, crop under & over keel the left ear

Robert Burfoots mark is under saw tooth the right ear crop slit & under keel the left ear

Susanah daughter of Andrew Stewart her mark is crop & under keel the left ear crop under & over keel the right ear

Jack Cornick his mark is over half crop the right ear & crop the left ear

John Masons mark is crop & slit the right ear crop under & over keel the left ear

William Wards mark is crop & slitt the right ear, under keel the left ear

William Dauley Senr his mark is crop & under half crop the right ear, crop & under saw tooth the left ear

~~Thomas Dauly~~ William Carrel Junr his mark is over slope & under saw tooth the right ear, crop the left ear

William Holmes his mark is crop under & over keel the left ear the right whole

William Edmonds his mark is a nick over the right ear & swallow fork the left ear

Eliz^a^ Woodhouse wid^o^ her mark is crop & slit the right ear & over keel the left ear

Hewlet Moseley his mark is under keel over keel & swallow fork the left ear the right ear whole

Charles James / son of ChaS / his mark is swallow fork the right ear & nick under the left ear

Wm Hancock Jun his mark is under saw tooth the right ear, crop & two slits the left ear

William Woodhouse Senr his mark is under keel & slit the right ear crop & two slitts the left ear

William Woodhouse son of Wm his mark is swallow fork & under keel the right ear & over half crop the left ear

Thorowgood Keelings mark is crop & over keel the left ear

Augt 14 David McClenahan mark is swallow fork & under keel the right ear & slit the left ear, which mark the said McClenahan bought of Anthy Whitehurst who married Amy Scott & gave him for it a heifer in presence of Arth Sayer this day

Thomas Lesters mark is crop & hole the left ear

William Shepard his mark is crop the right ear the left ear whole

Page c

Mr William Robinson mark is swallow fork the right ear & under saw tooth the left ear

1756 Feby Simon Stone his mark is swallow fork & nick over the left ear

James Gastons mark is two swallow forks & a hole in the right or left ear

Edward Bonney his mark is crop two slits & under keel the right ear & over keel the left ear

John Whichard his mark is crop & under keel the right ear the left ear whole

Robert / son of Robt Ward Junr his mark is crop the right ear & swallow fork the left ear

Horatio son of Edwd Daviss his mark is crop & hole both ears

Thomas Daulys mark is crop & under half crop the right ear

Charles Hartly his mark is crop & under half crop the right ear & slit the left ear

Joshua Matthias / son of Henry / his mark is crop & under keel the left ear

Robert Ward Junr son of Robt his mark swallow fork & over keel either ear & crop & hole the contrary ear

Robert Wards mark is crop & under half crop the right ear crop hole & under keel the left

Anthony Mundens mark is crop & over keel either ear & a hole the contrary ear

Francis Daviss her mark is swallow fork & over keel the left ear the right ear whole

John Hunters mark is under saw tooth the right ear crop & under keel the left ear

John Whitehurst / son of Simon / his mark is flower deluse above the right ear crop & flower deluse above the left

Dan[l] Whitehurst son of do his mark is crop & flower deluse above the right ear the left ear whole

M[s] Greshem Nimmo his mark is crop the left ear the right ear whole

George Stirings mark is crop & over keel the right ear & Flower deluce above the left ear

Elizabeth Burgess her mark is crop & under half crop the right ear & over keel the left ear

William Hunters mark is under keel either ear & nick under the contrary ear

John Smiths mark is slit & under keel the right ear & crop & over half crop the left ear

William Lovett / son of ThoS / his mark is flower deluse the right ear under half crop & under keel the left ear

Margret Wilbur her mark is crop & over half crop the left ear & slit the right ear

William Burgess / son of Henry / his mark is swallow fork under & over keel the right ear & under keel the left ear

M[s] Eliz[a] Walkes mark is crop & under slope the right ear & slit the left ear

Moses Cason his mark is over half crop left ear

James Cason son of James his mark is crop & under half crop the right ear & slit & under keel the left ear

John Cumbelford his mark is crop under & over keel the left ear & right ear whole

George Ball his mark is swallow fork the right ear crop slit under & over keel the left ear

Christian Alys mark is crop & a hole the right ear swallow fork & over keel the left ear

Adam Robertson his mark is crop hole & over keel the right ear crop hole under and over keel the left

Elizabeth Henly her mark is crop slit & under keel the right ear slit & over keel the left ear

Horatio Lands mark is crop & over keel the right ear

Luke Hills mark is crop & under half crop the right ear swallow fork & under keel the left ear

Lemuel Stone his mark is crop & over keel the right ear the left ear whole

Wm Daviss / son of Edw[d] / his mark is crop & under keel the right ear & crop the left ear

John Edmonds / son of Jn[o] / his mark is swallow fork & under keel the right ear

Henry Scotts mark is crop & under keel the right ear the left ear whole

Tully Wards mark is crop & under half crop the right ear crop & under keel the left ear

Francis Land / Jun his mark is crop & under keel the right ear the left ear whole

William Pettys mark is flower deluse the right ear crop slit & over keel the left ear

Nath[l] Land his mark is crop & nick under the right ear under keel & slit out the left ear

Daniel Grimsteads mark is under keel both ears

Page d

1757

May George Sparrow mark is crop & a hole the right ear under & over keel the left ear

Smith Sparrow his mark is swallow fork the right ear under half crop & slit out the left ear

June M[r] William Nimmos mark is crop & under half crop the left ear & slit out the right ear

The Rev[d] M[r] Robert Dicksons mark is crop under & over keel the right ear & over keel the left ear

George Ackiss's mark is crop & three slits the right ear & crop & slit the left ear

John Robertson / son of John / his mark is crop either ear crop hole & slit out the contrary ear

James Hills mark is crop & slit the right ear swallow fork & under keel the left ear

William Ashbys mark is crop & under keel the left ear & slit out the right ear

Edward Brown his mark is crop & two slits the right ear & under half crop the left ear

Maj[r] Thomas Walkes mark is swallow fork the right ear & under keel the left ear

Henry Consauls mark is crop & three slits the left ear

1758 Lewis Price his mark is under & over keel the right ear & crop the left ear

John Moores mark is croop the right ear & under saw tooth the left ear

Henry Keelings mark is swallow fork & under keel either ear & under keel & over slope the contrary ear

Edward Cannons mark is crop & slit the right ear crop under & over keel the left ear

John Morse Sen his mark is over half crop the right ear crop slit & under keel the left ear

Francis Morse his mark is crop slit & under keel the right ear & over half crop the left ear

John Hargrove his mark is slit the right ear & crop the left ear

John Pallets mark is crop the right ear under & over keel the left ear

Horatio Capps his mark is swallow fork & Flower deluce both ear

Keziah Robertson her mark is crop the right ear

Francis Morse mark is swallow fork the right ear & over saw tooth the left ear

George Norris / son of Thos / his mark is slit the right ear & crop & three slits the left ear

Mary Moore daughter of Ezekiel Moore her mark is crop slit & over keel the right ear & two nicks under the left

Mary Burroughs her mark is flower deluse the right ear & crop the left ear

Frederick Boush his mark is under & over keel the right ear crop & two slits the left ear

Abner Woodhouse his mark is swallow fork the right ear crop & three slits the left ear

Sarah Buskey wido her mark is crop slit & under keel the right ear slit & under keel the left ear

John Whitehurst / son of Emanuel / his mark is slit both ears & under keel the right ear

John Stone son of John Stone Jun his mark is slit both ears & under keel the right ear

1759 John Murden his mark is crop & under keel the right ear & slit the left ear

Mary Lovetts mark is crop & two slits the right ear slit out & flower deluse the left ear

Peter Whitehurst his mark is swallow fork & under keel the right ear crop & two slits the left ear

Christop Whitehurst his mark is crop & two slits the right ear swallow fork & under keel the left ear

Anna Ackiss her mark is crop slit & under keel the right ear & under slope the left ear

Fanne Ackiss her mark is crop & slit the right ear, under slope & over keel the left ear

John Ackiss mark is under slope the right ear, crop & slit the left ear

Batson Land his mark is crop & under half crop the right ear over crop & under keel the left ear

Jeremiah Murden his mark is crop & under keel the right ear & swallow fork the left ear

Hillary Whitehurst his mark is swallow fork & under keel the right ear & under keel the left ear

George Logans mark is crop the left ear & slit the right ear

John Williams's mark is crop & under half the right ear, over keel the left ear

James Dunns mark is swallow fork the right ear crop & slit the left ear

Col Edward Hack Moseleys mark is crop under & over keel both ears

Tully / son of Morris / Hill his mark is swallow fork & over keel the right ear & crop & slit the left ear

Charles Williamson son of Jas mark is crop under & over keel the right ear & crop the left ear

1760 Sewell Gasking his mark is crop & two slits the left ear the right ear whole

John Matthias's mark is crop & slit the right ear crop hole & under keel the left ear

Joel Edmonds his mark is swallow fork & under keel the right ear the left ear whole

Page e

1760 April Bette Morris (Jackson is written above Morris) her mark is crop the right ear & a hole in the left ear by her grandfather Jos Morris, Sen

Joel Peters his mark is flower deluce the right ear, crop & slit the left ear

James Eaton his mark is crop & slit the right ear & swallow fork the left ear

William Keeling his mark is a hole in the right ear swallow fork & nick under the left ear

William Capps his mark is crop the right ear & a hole in the left ear

Elias Roberts his mark is Fleur deluse the right ear slit & under keel the left ear

John Whiteharts mark is crop & under nick the right ear & crop & nick over keel the left ear

Francis Williamson his mark is under latch both ears

James Moore Jun his mark is crop & under keel the right ear crop & two slits the left ear

John Moore / son of Ja^{s} / his mark is slit the right ear crop & slit the left ear

Hezekiah Fentriss his mark is flower deluce the right ear swallow fork & nick over the left ear

William Woodhouse son of Phillip / his mark is crop & two slits the right ear & under keel the left ear

Phillip Disons mark is under saw tooth the right ear & over keel the left ear

Richard Bonneys mark is under keel the right ear the left ear whole

Jane Bonneys mark is crop & nick under the right ear & over keel the left ear

Robert Thorowgood his mark is crop & slit the right ear & crop the left ear

Henry Scott his mark is crop & under keel the left ear

Jacob Nimmos mark is crop & a hole the left ear, the right ear whole

Robert Moseleys mark is under & over keel the right ear, crop & slit the left ear which mark was given him by Capt George Wishart who recorded it in 1730

Francis Land son of Fra Thorowg^{d} Land decd / his mark is crop u& under keel the right ear & under keel the left ear

William Moseley Jun his mark is under keel the right ear, crop & under keel the left ear

Patrick Murphy Sen his mark is crop & slit the right ear & slit out the left ear

	John Wmson son of Geo. His mark is crop & under half crop the right ear & crop the left ear
	Richd Simmons his mark is under keel & slit out the right ear & under half crop the left ear
1761	Mr Thomas Ray^{s} Walker his mark is under saw tooth both ears & nick over either
	William Ackiss his mark is crop & slit the right ear & crop & two slits the left ear
	John Hancocks mark is under keel both ears & slit out either ear
	Jonathan Senica his mark is crop & under keel both ears
	James Carraway mark is crop & under slope both ears
	Wm Carraways mark is crop & under slope the right ear, crop & slit the left ear
	Henry Dudleys mark is crop & over half crop the right ear crop & under keel the left ear
	John Dudleys mark is crop & under keel the right ear crop & over half crop the left ear
	Francis Moores mark is over keel & slit the right ear & crop the left ear
Febry 17	William Pebworths mark is crop & a hole in each ear
	John Haynes Jun his mark is crop under half crop & slit the right ear over slope and under keel the left ear
	Joseph Ottersons mark is under half crop the right ear crop & under keel the left ear
	Cornelius Lamounts mark is crop slit & over keel the right ear swallow fork & under keel the left ear
	Willoughby Buskeys mark is crop the right ear crop & slit the left ear
	Charles Norriss' mark is crop & two slits the right ear, slit & flower deluce the left ear
	John Smiths mark is crop & two slits the right ear & swallow fork the left ear
	Charles Dickenson his mark is crop & over keel the right ear crop & under half crop the left ear
	Francis Moores mark is over keel the right ear & crop the left ear
June 20	William Keeling son of John / his mark is crop & two slits the right ear over keel & nick under the left ear
	Adam Robertson Jun his mark is crop the right ear the left ear whole
	William Godfry mark is swallow fork the right ear crop & two slits the left ear
	Wm Nimmo his mark given him by Charles Nicholson crop and under half crop in the left ear and hole in the right ear
	Charles Nicholson's mark is over keel both ears & under keel the left ear
January 1762	James Powers mark is croop & under keel & whole the right & crop & two slits the left

Martha Bakers mark is swallow fork & over keel the left ear & slitt the right

John Fen tresses mark is swallow fork the left ear & flower de louse the right

Page f

1762 January	Henry Lovet son of Thomas his mark crop the right ear & two nicks over Flower de louse the left
	Thomas Hunter Junr his mark under keel either ear & under saw tooth the other
	John Pallet Junr his mark is staple fork the right ear crop slit & under keel the left ear
Feby 15th	William Dudley's mark is under saw tooth the right ear & crop & two slits the left ear. Bought of Leml Newton
May 14	Miss Frankie Walke her mark is crop & under slope the right ear & slit out the left which mark was given her by Capt Williamson
	Mr. Nathaniel Danby's mark is crop whole under keel the right & croop whole under nick the left
	Lowery Powers mark is crop the left ear
	George Collins's mark is over keel the left ear and slit the right ear reded this 20th day of March 1765
July 4th 1762	Mr. Borrough Moseley's mark is crop & under half crop the let ear which mark was sold him by Henry Snaile
July 20	Mr. Perrin Smyths mark is over saw tooth the right ear crop and slitt the left
	Miss Molley Walkes mark is crop the left ear slit neck over & under slope the right ear
	Mr Peter Singletons mark is slitt & over neck the right ear & under keel the left
October 1762	Mr. William Robinson son William / his mark is swallow fork the left ear & under saw tooth the right
	Ann Robinsons mark is under saw tooth both ears
	Mr. Nathaniel Fentrises mark is crop the right and whole and slit the left which mark was given him by his grandmother
Decemr 29	Mr. James Shearwood mark is crop & under keel the left ear and over keel the right which said mark was his fathers
	Anthony James his mark is swallow fork and over keel the left ear and slit the right
Janry 1763	Walter Lyon his mark is under saw tooth the right ear slit & under keel the left ear
May 30	Thomas James's mark is crop and under half crop the left and crop the right

Jul 15 — Margaret Thorowgood her mark is crop the right ear & under saw tooth & under keel the left ear which said mark was her husbands

Augt 2^{d} — M^{r}. John Thorowgood Junr his mark is crop & slitt the right ear and over keel & under saw tooth the left ear

James Whitehurst mark is swallow fork & under keel the right ear and crop the left

Elizabeth Sayer her mark is slitt the left ear & under keel the right ear

Charles Sayer his mark is slitt the right ear and under keel the left

Page g

1763

Septem 28th — Henry Capps crop and two under nicks the left and slit the right

October 27 — Nathaniel Keelings crop & slitt the right ear which said mark was James Harrisons deced

1764

January 10 — Ann Cunsaulvo her mark is crop & three slits the left ear which said mark was her fathers

John Murry's mark is slitt the right ear & crop & two slits the left ear

John Parsons alias Scady his mark is slitt & crop both ears

February 20 — Peter Nolley Ellegoods mark is swallow fork the right ear & under keel & over keel the left ear

Robert Holmes's mark is crop under keel & over the right ear

Jacamine Attwood's mark is swallow fork both ears & under keel both

Solomon Frizzels mark is crop both ears & under half crop the left ear

April 1st — James Hartgrove's mark is crop the left ear and over half crop the right ear

Solomon Creeds mark is crop & two slits the right and slit out the left

John Creeds mark is crop & saw tooth the right and slit out the left

10th — John Shepherd's mark is crop the right ear

Maximilian Boushes mark is under keel both ears & under sloops both ears

13th — John Killy's mark is croop both & over keel the right

14th — John Simmons / son of Richard his mark is swallow & under keel the left & crop & hole the left

20th — Edward James / son of John / his mark is crop the left ear and crop the right ear

25th — John Lovett / son of John / his mark is crop slitt & over keel the right and flower deluse the left ear

September 13th	Mrs Elizabeth Hunters mark is under keel either ear & under nick either
October 13	Simon Jackson's mark is crop the right ear & under keel & over keel the left ear
	James Jackson Jr his mark is under keel the right ear & over keel the left ear
25	Thos. Harrison / son of Henry / his mark crop & slit the left ear, over keel & nick under the right ear
	John Lewis / son of Thomas Lewis / his mark is crop the left ear
30	John Stone jun. his mark is crop and staple fork the right ear

Page h

1764	
Novemr 10th	Henry Trower his mark is slitt both ears
Decemr 11	William Flear his mark is over half crop both ears
25th	John Gornto his mark is crop and three slits the right and whole in the left ear
	Ruben Gornto his mark is crop and a whole the left ear and over half crop the right ear
1765	
January 2d	James Williamson his mark is crop the right ear & crop under & over keel the left ear
10th	Anthony Lovett his mark is crop and slit the right & Flower deluse the left ear
	Jacob Ellegoods mark is crop slitt under and over keel either ear
February 15th	Henry Whites mark is crop and over keel either ear and whole the other
	Robert Ballard's mark is crop and slitt the right ear & under sloope the left ear
	Katherine Dearmore her mark is crop and two slits the right ear & a hole the left ear
	Honour Dearmore her mark is under keel the left ear
16th	William Whitehurst / son of Anthº / his mark is crop both ears & under keel the left ear
	Burrough Moseleys mark is crop and two slits the right ear and crop and under half crop the left ear
Apr 6th	William Stone son of Lemuel Stone his mark is swallow fork and under keel the right ear and flower deluce the left ear
	Nathan Munden's mark is swallow fork the right ear & crop and two slits the left
May 21st	John Stone his mark is swallow fork and under keel the right ear and Flower de luce the left ear
	William Brock son of Thomas his mark is swallow fork the left and crop and saw tooth the right ear

July 16th	Abner Malbone / son of James Malbone / his mark is under half crop either ear
August 11th	David Barret's mark is crop both ears over nick the right ear and under nick the left ear
	Martha Keeling's mark is crop both ears
September 11th	Lemuel Newtons mark is crop & under half crop the left ear & under keel the right ear which said mark was my fathers
October 16	Elizabeth Nimmo's mark is crop and over half crop the right swallow fork and under keel the left
Novemr 28	Simon Senaca son of John his mark is crop & slit both ears & under keel the right
30	Jeremiah Broughton's mark croop & two slits the left & nick under the right ear
1766	
January 30th	Moses Brown / son of Hezikiah Brown / his mark is crop and hole the right and crop and slit the left

Page i

1766	
February 1	Francis Woodhouse's mark crop & three slits the left ear half crop the right ear
March 23d	William Henley's mark is crop & whole the right crop slitt under keel & over keel the left ear
Apl 10th	Maximilian Boush's mark is slit the right ear & over sloope & under keel the left ear
May 8th	William Brock his mark is slit the right ear & over sloope & under keel the left ear
13th	John Taner's mark is crop the left ear, slit and under keel the right ear
15	Solomon Cason, son of James, his mark is under keel the left ear
August 16th	Thomas Owens's mark is crop & slit the left & hole the right ear
	Idem mark is crop and over keel the right under and over keel the left ear
October 11th	Tully Moore's mark is crop and under saw tooth the right and under half crop the left ear
30th	Lynhaven Parish's mark is swallow fork the right ear & under & over keel the left ear
	John Bishop his mark is slitt the right ear
November	Edward Davis his mark is swallow fork and under keel the left ear
Decemr	James Davis's mark is crop and under the right crop & whole the left ear
	William Otterson's mark is crop & whole the right & under saw tooth the left ear
1767	
April 28	Hillory Moseleys mark is swallow fork the left ear

May 7th	William Dawley son Wm. his mark is crop and under half crop the right crop and saw tooth the left ear
Sepr 22	Moses Bonney's mark is crop and under and over keal boath ears
October 5	John Kenlines mark is crop and three slits the right ear & crop & slit the left ear
Decemr 19th	Edward Petta his mark is swallow fork both ears and a hole in the right
1768	
March 26th	Amey Cox her mark is swallow fork the left ear and under keal the right ear
April 12th	Thomas Ward Junr his mark is crop & under half crop the right Flower deluce the left ear
April 26th	Elizabeth Keeling her mark is over slope the right ear & under slope the left ear
May 4	Henry Edwards mark is crop and over keel the right ear, and under half crop the left ear
	William Robinson (son of William deceased) his mark is swallow fork the right ear and under saw tooth the left ear
9th	Nicholas Griffin his mark is slit the right ear and crop the left ear
14	George Wishart Junr his mark is swallow fork the left ear and over keal the right
21	John Haynes Junr his mark is crop and under half crop and slitt the left ear, over slope and under keel the right ear

Page j

July 1d 1768	William Benthall his mark is swallow fork the left and over keal the right ear
October 13th	Dennis Dawley / son of Dennis Gent. / crop & half crop the left ear and under keel the right
	Amey Dawley / daughter of Dennis Dawley Gent. / under half crop the left and under saw tooth the right
Novemr 18th	William McClenahan his mark is crop and under and over keal either ear and slit either ear
1769	
January 2d	Jonathan Jackson's mark is under keel both ears and slitt both ears
April 8th	William Keeling, son of Wm. his mark is slit out the right and hole the left ear
22d	Thomas Langley / son of Thomas Langley / his mark is crop and under half crop the left ear & nick over the left ear
May 18th	John Saunders his mark is under half crop the left and under keel the right ear
	Joshua James (son of Edward) his mark is crop and under slope the right ear

	John Williams (son of John) his mark is crop and under half crop the right & left ear
	John Snail j^{r} his mark is crop and under half crop the right ear
31st	Charles Matthias / son of Henry / his mark is crop and under half crop both ears
	Lemuel Thorowgood his mark is crop hole and slit out the right under keal the left ear
June 8th	Thomas Hunter / son of John / his mark is crop the right and under saw tooth and over keel the left
	David Carraway / son of James / his mark is crop and under slope the left ear and slitt out the right
	Jonathan Carraway / son of James / his mark is crop and under slope the left ear and swallow fork the right
20th	Ruben Matthias / son of Henry / his mark is crop and slitt the left & under keel the right
26	Mary James widow & relict of Charles James her mark is crop & under keel either ear & under half crop the contrary
28	James Williamson Senr his mark is crop both ears & under slope the left ear
July 17	Anthony Walke his mark is swallow fork the right ear & a hole in the left ear
	Ditto under half crop the right & swallow fork the left ear
25	Henry Cornick / son of Henry / mark is crop the right ear and over half crop and slit in the under side of the left ear
August 3^{d}	William Griffin / son of John / mark is swallow fork & under keel the left ear & slitt the right at length
22	Adam Keeling / son of Thomas / his mark is under keel the left ear & over slope the right ear
October 28th	Reuben Wiles, son of Thos Wiles deceased, his mark is crop and half crop the left ear the right ear whole
Novr 2	Willm Attwood, son of Edward, mark is crop & under keel the left ear & swallow fork the right
25	William Keeling, son of William mark is slit one ear and a hole in the other
	Francis Keeling / son of W^{m} / mark is crop slitt & under keel the right ear & over slope and under keel the left ear
	Robert Keeling / son of W^{m} /mark is over slope and under keel the left ear and crop slitt and under keel the right ear
26	Solomon Waterman, son of Charles, mark is crop & two slits the right & under keel the left ear
Decem^{r} 1st	John Gardoner, mark is under saw tooth the left ear & under half crop the right ear
1770	William White mark slitt the left ear & under keel the right

John Bonney / son of John Senr / crop & nick the right & slit & under keel the left ear

William May son of William mark's swallow fork the right ear & crop slitt & under keel the left

Francis (unreadable)tty (possibly Petty) son of Edwd marks crop both ears and under and over keel both ears

Francis Leggets marks crop & over half crop the right & crop & under half crop the left ear

Page k

Sept 5th 1770	Martha Nimmo, widow of Wm Nimmo, her mark is crop and half crop the left ear and a hole in the right
October 30th	Margaret Moseley daughter of Wm Moseley, Gent her mark crop & under slope the right ear & slitt out the left
January 10th 1771	Martha Brinson Widow of William Brinson her mark is crop both ears and saw tooth under and over
January 10th 1771	Jamima Moore daughter of William Brinson her mark is crop the left ear and two cuts under the right
January 11th 1771	Nathan Carrel son of William his mark is over slope and under saw the right ear and crop the left ear
January 11th 1771	Mary Carrel widow of William Carrel deceased her mark is crop both ears and under keel both and a hole in each
February the 11th	Joshua Hopkins his mark is crop the left ear a slit and under keel and the right ear under keel
February 11th 1771	Elizabeth Hopkins Widow of John her mark is under square both ears
March 4th 1771	Charles Nicholson his mark is crop and under slope the left ear and swallow fork the right ear
March 4th 1771	David Etheridge his mark is under half crop both ears
April 26th 1771	Thomas Norriss his mark is crop and two slits in the left ear and a slit on the right ear
June 4th 1771	William Strawbridge his mark is crop and under keel the right ear swallow fork and flower deluce the left ear
June 6th 1771	Anne Cornick widow of Henry her mark is crop the left ear and over half crop the right ear and under slit
July 4th 1771	Mr. William Aitchison his mark is crop slit and under keel the right ear crop and under keel the left it is Mr Weblin's mark

July the 20th	Margaret Willis widow of John Willis her mark is crop and three slits in the left ear, and a nick under the right ear
November 2d	Richard Wilbur, son of William, his mark is crop and over half crop the right ear and under saw tooth the left ear
January 3d 1772	Cornelius Brinson, son of Richard, his mark is a crop and hole in the right ear and a crop and three slits in the left ear & was the said Richard's mark
February 9th 1772	Capt George Scott his mark is crop and under half crop both ears
April 14th 1772	Tully Cason, son of James Cason, his mark is crop and half crop the left ear slit and under keel the right ear, and is the same mark that his grandmother lately had

Page 1

1772

May 12th	Adam Keeling his mark is crop the left ear and a hole in the right ear
	Henry Keeling his mark is under slope the right ear and over slope the left ear
July 10th 1772	Joab Wright his mark is a crop and hole in the right ear, over keel and under saw tooth the left ear, and is the same mark which his father had
July 29	Robert Trower, son of Henry, his mark is slit out both ears
September 10th	Jonathan James, son of Jonathan, his mark is crop and under keel the right ear and crop the left ear and is the mark that was his father's
Octo 1772 25th	George Gasking, son of Charles decd. his mark is crop and slit the left ear
December 8th 1772	Henry Gaskins, son of Henry, his mark is crop and two slits in the left ear, and under keel both ears
December 22 1772	Thos Bank his mark is over keel under keel crop both ears & slit the right ear

1773

January 5th	John Absalom: son of Edmund: his mark is swallow fork the right ear, crop, slit, & under keel the left ear
March 12th	William Huggins, son of Robert decd., his mark is slit on the right, and under half crop the left ear, which was the said Robert's mark
22d March	John Cason, son of John, his mark is crop and half crop the left ear and slit out and under keel the right ear, and is the same mark that Tully Cason had recorded last April: who consented & let the said John Cason have the same: he having one that he liked better
April 6th	Henry Matthias, son of John, his mark is crop the left ear and under keel, and two nicks over the right ear
May 17th	John Etheridge, Tailor, his mark is under half crop the right ear and slit the left ear and an under bit in the left

May 17th	William Walker, overseer, his mark is under half crop left ear and slit the right ear and an under bit in the right

Page m

1773

May 26th	Robinson Smith, his mark is under saw tooth the right ear crop and two slits in the left ear
August 23d	James Carril, son of William, his mark is over slope and under saw tooth the right ear, & crop the left ear ------ which was his brother Nathans mark
August 24th	Mrs Betty Moseley widow of Mr William Moseley decd her mark is crop and over keel the left ear and under keel the right her said husband's mark
August 24th	Margaret Moseley daughter of William Moseley Gent decd, her mark is crop and under slope the right ear and slit the left which was her said fathers mark
August 24th	Francis Land, son of Francis Thorowgood Land, his mark is under keel both ears and crop the left which said mark belonged to William Mosely Gent
August 28th	Isaac Totewenc, his mark is crop and slit the right and under keel the left ear
Sept 11th	William Pebworth, his mark is under slope the right ear under keel and over slope the left ear which was the mark that Henry Woodhouse had
5th Novr	Anne Norris widow of Charles, her mark is crop and two slits in the right ear, slit and flower deluce the left ear which was the sd Charles mark
	John Forrest, son of John decd. his mark is crop and a hole in the left hcar
6th Novr	Ebenezer Craig's mark is crop and slit under keel the right ear and swallow fork the left
10th Decr	Tully Moseley, son of Hillary, his mark is crop the right or left ear and over square the other on both ears and it's the same mark that his grandfather had who lately departed this life

Page n

1773

Decr 15th	John James, son of William, his mark is crop the right ear swallow fork the left
Decr 15th	William James, son of John, his mark is crop the left ear and a slit under and over keel the right ear and is the same mark which his grandfather Robt Moseley had and gave to him
Decr 30th	Edward Hack Moseley Junr his mark is swallow fork the right ear and slit the left
Decr 30th	William Robinson Gent son of Capt Tully Robinson his mark is saw tooth the right ear and crop the left
Decr 30th	Joshua Whitehurst, son of Capt Whitehurst, his mark is slit out both ears and under keel the left ear

Decr 30th	Mr James Robinson his mark is crop and slit the right ear and under slope the left ear is the mark that Capt Robert Ballard had
Decr 30th	Mr Tully Robinson his mark is saw tooth both ears and is the mark that Anne Robinson had
Decr 31st	Mr Tully Robinson his mark is saw tooth and slit down the right ear and crop the left
1774	
January 13th	John Whitehurst son of Joshua his mark is slit out both ears and under keel the right
January 15th	William Hunter, son of James, his mark is crop and slit the right ear and under saw tooth the left which was his fathers mark
Febr 1774	Richard Land his mark is crop and two slits in the right ear and a hole in the left
March 25	George Shore his mark crop and over keel the right ear and a hole in the left which was John Mungumrys mark
March28th	James Holmes, son of William, his mark is crop and under keel and over keel the left ear

Page o

1774	
March 28th	Edward James an infant son of Mr Edward James, his mark is swallow fork and under keel the right ear and swallow fork the left ear which was Capt Lamounts mark
March 28th	John James son of Mr. Edward James his mark is crop and under slope the right ear and crop the left
April 4th	James Pebworth, son of Henry, his mark is crop and a hole in the right and swallow fork the left ear
April 4th	William Pebworth son of William his mark is swallow fork both ears and an under nick in the right ear
14th April	Jonathan Woodhouse Junr his mark is crop and two slits in the left ear slit and under keel the right was Captt Wm Woodhouse's mark
June 6th	Sarah Huggins widow of Nathaniel Huggins her mark is swallow fork the left ear crop and over keel the right ear and was the said Nathaniels mark
June 24th	John Banks, son of Harrison, his mark is over keel and under keel and crop both ears and slit the right ear which was his father's mark
June 24th	Isaac Jacobs his mark is crop and two slits on the right ear and slit the left ear
June 24th	Caleb Whitehurst, son of Richard, his mark is crop and two swallow forks in the right ear
July 13	John McClenahan his mark is swallow fork and under keel either ear and slit either ear which was Mr David McClenahan's mark
Sept 20th	Charles Robinson his mark is crop and over keel the right ear and crop and under half crop the left ear
Sept 20th	Jonathan Scopus his mark is crop and under keel the right ear and a hole in the left ear

Page p

1774	
Oct^{o} 31st	Thomas Drewry his mark is under and over keel the right ear with a slit in the same
Decr 5th	Caleb Lamount his mark is swallow fork each ear which was his father Henry Lamounts mark
Decr 5th	Frances Lamount widow of Henry Lamount dec^{d} her mark is crop and over half crop the right ear crop and under half crop the left ear
Decr 19th	Capt Tully Robinson his mark is under square both ears
1775	
January 16th	John Buskey son of Jonathan his mark is crop a hole and over keel the left ear & crop the right ear
March 20th	Mrs Sarah Lyon her mark is saw tooth the right ear slit and under keel the left ear
April 10th	Thomas Henley son of Charles his mark is crop and slit each ear
April 10th	Henry Henley son of Charles his mark is crop and two slits each ear
May 10th	Capt Lemuel Cornick his mark is crop and slit one ear and over the slope the other ear it was his fathers mark
May 10th	John Woodhouse, son of John, his mark is crop & slit the right ear and under keel both ears, it was his fathers mark
May 11th	Zekel Moore, son of Caleb Moore, his mark is crop and a hole in the right ear & crop under and over keel the left ear
August 14th	Anne Barnes, widow of Anthony, her mark is under half crop the right ear, slit and under keel the let ear
1776	
Jan^{ry} 30th	Elizabeth Haynes, widow of John Haynes, her mark is slit and under half crop the right ear, over slope and under keel the left ear
Jan^{ry} 30th	William Haynes, son of John, his mark is slit and under half crop the left ear, over slope and under keel the right ear
Jan^{ry} 30th	Susanna Barnes, daughter of Henry, her mark is crop and under keel both ears

Page q

1776	
Feb^{r} 12th	Joshua Cannon son of Thomas his mark is swallow fork the right ear slit and over keel the left ear
Feb^{r} 12th	William Cannon son of Thomas his mark is crop under keel & a hole in the left ear & crop the right ear
April 11th	Mr James Nimmo his mark is swallow fork the right ear and slit the left

April 11th	Mr Paul Proby his mark is swallow fork the left ear and slit the right
June 26th	Hillary son of Ree Land, his mark is crop and over keel the right ear & slit out the left which was Betty Shipps mark
July 30th	Mrs Amy Dickson her mark is crop under keel & over keel the right ear and over keel the left which was the Rev Mr Robert Dickson's mark
13th August	James Smith his mark is crop and over half crop and a nick in the under part of the left ear and slit out the right ear
24th August	John James Junr son of Edward James, his mark is swallow fork & under keel the right ear & swallow fork the left ear
Novr 9th	John Oliver his mark is crop & under slope each ear & was James Carraways mark
Novr 14th	Amy Ashby widow of William her mark is crop & under keel the left ear & slit the right ear at length
Novr 14th	James Carraway Junr his mark is crop & under slope each ear & was his uncles mark
1777	
April	Henry Cornick son of Joel his mark is under saw tooth the right ear and slit on the left ear
March 13th	John Cox son of William his mark is slit the right ear slit nick under & over the left ear
May 20th	Matthew Pallett son of John his mark is under keel & over keel the left ear and crop the right & was his father's mark
Ditto	John Pallett son of John his mark is under keel & over keel the right ear and crop the left & was his father's second mark
Ditto	William Pallett son of John his mark is under keel & over keel the left ear and crop & slit the right & was his father's third mark

Page r

1777	
June 9th	Landfare Burgess his mark is crop & under half crop the right ear and over keel the left & was Jno Williams's mark
June 9th	Nathaniel Nimmo son of William his mark is half under crop right ear slit the left and under keel the left ear
June 9th	Mr John Tipling his mark is swallow fork the right ear crop slit and under keel the left ear & was Jno Absalom's mark
Jun 17th	James Carraway, son of Wm, his mark is crop and under slope the left ear and slit out the right ear & was his father's mark
June 17th	Wm Carraway son of James Carraway his mark is crop & under staple both ears & slit the left
July the 12th	William Hill his mark is crop and slit the right ear and swallow fork and under keel the left

July 12th	Joseph Hill his mark is swallow fork and under keel the right ear & swallow fork and over keel the left
Octo 15th	James Tenant his mark is slit the right ear & under saw tooth the left & was his grandfather Hunter's mark
Novr 7th	Kiziah Stone daughter of John, her mark is crop the right ear & under keel the left
Decr 3d	Thos West Junr son of Thos his mark is swallow fork & under keel both ears
Decr 19th	George Broughton his mark is crop & two slits under and over keel the right ear & crop & two slits in the left
1778	
Janry 8th	Thomas Robinson son of Adam his mark is crop the right ear & a hole in the left
17th	Adam Lovet Son of James Lovet, his mark is crop & over keel the left ear & Flower deluce the right
	John Lovet, son of James Lovet, his mark is crop slitt over keel the right ear
Febr 17th	James Wilbur his mark is crop & over half crop the right ear & slit the left
March	Margaret Lovet, daughter of Reuben, her mark is crop & two slits in the right ear & under keel the left & was the mark of William Woodhouse son of Philip
March	Elihu Moore his mark is swallow fork both ears & a nick in the left
March	Polly Moore, daughter of Elihu, her mark is swallow fork both ears & a nick in the right
Octo 8th	Rebecca Buskey her mark is crop both ears and slit the left

Page s

1778	
April 21th	Thomas Stone son of Simon Stone his mark is crop & three slits in the left ear and a hole in the right and is the mark that John Henley Junr had
April 28th	William Norriss his mark is under slope the right ear and flower deluce the left ear
April 28th	William Cartwright his mark is swallow fork the left ear & crop under slope the right
April 28th	William Gasking son of George his mark is crop & slit the right ear
May 17th	John Carraway his mark is swallow fork & under keel both ears
20th	Endiniam Cornick his mark is a hole in the right ear and a slit in the left & was William Keeling Junr mark
21st	Moses Land, son of Edwd, his mark is crop & over keel the right ear & over keel the left
3d June	Thos Raney his mark is crop and swallow fork under part of the right ear
Ditto	William Raney son of Thos his mark is crop and swallow fork the under part of the left ear
11th June	Sarah Roberts her mark is slit & under keel the left ear and flower deluce the right

18th June	Ree Land son of Ree, his mark is crop & over half crop the right ear and slit & over keel the left ear
July 3d	James Braithwaite his mark is a hole in each ear
10th	Tully Williamson Junr his mark is swallow fork the left ear and a hole in each ear
Augst 13th	William Whitehead, son of John, his mark is crop and under nick the right ear & crop the left ear
Augst 21st	Ezekiel Cox his mark is crop & slit the right ear and a hole in the left ear
22d	Henry Burgess's mark is crop & slit the left ear & swallow fork the right ear
	Thos Burgess son of Henry his mark is swallow fork the left ear and under keel both ears
Sept 1st 1778	David Huggins his mark is crop the right ear, over & under keel the left & was Doctr Price's mark

Page t

June	John Whitehurst his mark is under half crop & nick under the left ear only
1753 Janry	John Mundens mark is crop the right ear crop & under half crop the left ear
	Adam Keeling Senr his mark is crop the left ear & a hole in the right hear
	Zacharias Boush his mark is crop & over half crop the right ear slit & under keel the left ear
Febry	Sarah Simmons wido her mark is crop & half flower deluse the upper part of the right ear swallow fork & under keel the left ear
	Wm Harper son of John / his mark is crop & over keel the right & left ear
	Andrew Consauls mark is crop & slit the left ear & nick under the right ear
	Charles Smallwood his mark is flower deluse & slit both ears
March	John Muntgomery his mark is crop & over keel the right ear & a hole in the left ear
	James Williamson his mark is crop the right ear crop and under slope the left ear
	Frances Pelree wido her mark is flower de luse the right ear crop and slit the left ear
April	John Maye his mark is swallow fork the right ear crop & under keel the left ear
	George Jamesons mark is crop & two slits the right ear crop & staple fork the left ear
	Joshua Lands mark is crop & slit the right ear crop the left ear
	James Lands mark is crop slit & under keel the right ear & a while in the left
	Hillary Brown's mark is crop & two slits the right ear & under half crop the left ear
	William Wrights mark is crop & nick under the right ear, the left ear whole
	James Wrights mark is crop & nick under the left ear the right ear whole
	John Consauls mark is crop & three slits the right ear the left ear whole
May 11	Charles James mark is crop & under keel either ear & under half crop the contrary

Erasmus Haynes's mark is crop & flower deluce the right ear & under half crop the left ear

John Griffins mark is under saw tooth & over keel the right ear & under and over keel the left ear

Betty Hill her mark is two swallow forks the right ear & swallow fork the left ear

John Pallets mark is crop & two slits both ears

Thorowgood Capps mark is crop & under saw tooth the right ear & under saw tooth the left ear

26 John Brock son of Wm his mark is crop & slit the right ear crop & under half crop the left ear

Capt Samuel Tenants mark crop slit & under keel both ears

William Biddles mark is swallow fork the right ear slit & over keel the left

June 22 James Lovetts mark is Flower deluce the right ear crop & nick over the left ear

Thos Lovetts his mark is flower deluce the right ear crop & two nicks over the left

James Lovett Junr his mark is flower deluce the right ear crop & over keel the left ear

Robert Williamson son of Bartho his mark is crop & over keel the right ear crop & under slope the left ear

George Gasking his mark is swallow fork & under keel the right ear & a hole in the left ear

John Gordans mark is a hole in the right ear swallow fork & under keel the left ear

Bette Henly her mark is crop under keel & a hole the right ear over keel & a hole the left

Joseph White his mark is over slope & nick under the right ear & under slope the left ear

Page 1

Ano 1691 Patrick Angus SenE his mark swallow fork & under keel the right eare under keel & over keel the left

James Angus his mark swallow fork & under keel the right eare over keel & saw tooth under the left

Patrick Angus JunE his mark swallow fork & under keel the right eare under keel & saw tooth over the left

Florentius Porter his mark crop the left eare & saw tooth under the right

Sarah Woodhouse her mark half crop over the left eare & a rounding piece under & halfe crop under the right

Horatio Woodhouse his mark crop & slitt the left eare half crop over the right & a rounding piece under each

John Macarty his mark slitt & a nick under the right eare, crop & two nicks under the left

Thomas Webb his mark swallow fork the right eare & half crop over the left

Richard Cox his mark swallow fork & under keel the right eare & half crop over the left

George Marsh Sen^e^ his mark crop & hole the right eare & saw tooth the left

George Marsh Jun^e^ his mark crop both eares & two holes in each eare

Alexander Wylie his mark flower deluce the right eare & half crop under the left

John Jones his mark swallow fork the right eare & slitt the left of which mark he hath one cow and cow yearling given him by his grandfather Thomas Morris, and another cow & cow yearling given him by his father Edward Jones with their increase both male & female

Thomas Williams his mark crop & half crop both eares & a slitt in the uppermost halfe of the right eare

Thomas Spratt his mark crop, hole & under keell the right eare, crop & two slits the left

Robert Vaughan his mark crop slitt & under keell both ears & two nicks in each under keel

Henry Southern his mark two swallow forks & a nick under the right eare

Richard Jones his mark flower deluce the left ear crop hale & under keel the right

Richard Capps his mark crop the right eare & two pieces taken out under both eares

William Grant his mark crop & flower deluce the left eare crop & swallow fork the right

James Fitzgerrald his mark crop & under keell both eares

William Fitzgerrald his mark swallow fork the right eare & over keell the left

Hannah Ward her mark crop & two slitts the left ear & the right eare whole

William Newport his marke swallow fork & under keell both eares

John Sullivan Jun^E^ his mark under keell the right eare, hole & slitt out the left

Adam Thorowgood his mark crop the right eare & over keell the left

Thomas Lovett his mark slitt the right eare crop slitt & flower deluce the left

Thomas Franklin his mark swallow fork and under keell the right eare & two swallow forks the left

Margaret Makeell her mark crop & over keell the right eare & swallow fork the left

Thomas Bodnam his mark crop both eares slitt both eares & under keell the right

Richard Smith his mark crop slitt & under keell the right eare crop slitt & over keell the left

Thomas Webb is mark crop & two slitts the right eare under keell & hole the left

John Brown his mark swallow fork the right eare crop & two slitts the left

William Boggs his mark swallow fork the right eare half crop under the left

John Vaughan his mark crop both eares two slitts in the right & one in the left

Beniamin Cumming his mark crop both eares & two slitts in each eare

Francis Morse his mark crop & slitt & under keell the left eare & half crop over the right

Robert Thorowgood his mark swallow fork the right eare & under keell the left

Henry Walstone his mark half crop under the left eare & slit the right

Richard Smith Jun^{E} half crop under the left eare & two slitts in the right

James Cason his mark slitt both eares & under keell the right

Elizabeth Cason her mark slitt both eares & under keell the left

John Gisborne his mark crop both eares & a hole in each eare

Susanna Gisborne her mark crop both eares a hole in each eare & a nick under the right

Hannah Cook widow her marke two over keels & a slitt under the right eare

Richard Cook his mark over keell & a nick cut out under the left eare crop & half crop the right eare

Anthony Cook his mark two over keels & two under keels

Hannah Cook Jun^{E} her mark two over keels & a nick taken out under the left eare

Margaret Frisell widow her mark over keell & a nick under the right eare crop & under keel the left

Martin Cornick his mark crop & two slitts the left eare and halfe crop the right

Page 2

1691 Sep^{E} 2^{d}	John Fulcher Jun^{E} his mark crop & slitt both eares of which mark he hath a cow & a heifer the originall of which cattle was given to him by his Aunt Elizabeth Oakeham
1701 9^{ber} 5th	Wm Fentris his mark slitt in ye right eare down to ye middle & ye upper cut of close to the root & ye left eare slit down to ye middle to ye root
1702 Ap^{Ell} 11th	Richard Jones Shomaker Little Creek his mark two swallow forks & he sayth he have had ye same ye eleven years without any let
1702 May 2^{d}	Coll Edw: Moseleys son Hyllary Moseley mark being croop ye left eare & under keel the right wch mark was his grandfathers
1702	Robt Vahans mark is a slit in each eare & under keel ye left
1702	Eliz^{E} Fitzpatrick mark is swallow fork ye right & swallow fork & under keel ye left
1702	Jno Jones for James Smith mark is swallow fork left & slitt ye right
7^{ber} 1702	Wm Bond mark is two swallow fork left ear & over keel ye right
8b^{E} 1702	Mary Tooly's mark is swallow fork & a nick under ye left ear crop & ½ crop ye right
Novemb^{E} 1702	Richd Eiland Jun^{E} mark is under & over keel ye rite ear & crop & slitt & under keel ye left eare
Feb^{E} 1702/3	John Cockruft mark is croop & hole in ye left ear under keel & over keel ye right
Febrary 1702/3	Geo: Mattux mark is swallow fork ye right ear & popler leafe ye left
	Mickell Fentriss Jun^{E} his mark is swallow fork ye left eare croop & halfe croop ye right eare
Aprill ye 23: 1703	Thomas Wiles his mark is swallow fork the right eare croop and halfe croop the left ear

April 28 1703	Moses Fentris his mark is swall: fork & a nick in ye upper part of ye left eare & flower deluse ye right eare
D^o	Aron Fentris his mark is swall: fork & a nick in ye under part ye left eare & flow: deluse & slitt ye right eare
D^o	Rebecca Shurley her mark is croop and two slitts in ye left ear
1703	
June ye 26th	Mary Woodhouse daughter of M^E Henry Woodhouse decd, her mark is under keel & a piece taken out over ye right eare almost like ye half croop & croop & two slitts ye left
July ye 27th	Francis Moseley son of Wm Moseley mark is croop ye right ear
D^o	Mary Moseley daughter of D^o: Moseley mark is croop ye right ear & slitt in ye croop
D^o	Arthur Moseley son of D^o. Wm Sen^E mark is croop ye right ear & two slitts in ye croop
August ye 16th	John Webbling his mark is ye right eare under keele & a slitt in ye left ear under keele & over keele
Augth ye 30th	William Moore ye son of Morgan Moore his marke is slitt ye right & left eare which mark was his grandfathers
Aug y^{e}30th	Wm Moore son of Wm Moore of ye E: Shore his marke is swallow fork ye left eare & a peace from under & over ye same & under keele ye right eare & a peace taken out of ye upper & lower part ye same eare
D^o	Eliz^a Moore ye daughter of ye sd Wm Moore her marke is under keel ye right & left eare & a hole in the left eare
Y^e 29th 1703	Sarah Franklin ye daughter of Simon Franklin Sen^e her mark is swall^o: fork ye right & left eare
10b^r ye 16th	Thomas Heath his marke is cropp & slitt ye righte are & under keel & over keel ye left eare
Ye 21st	Sarah Fentris ye daug: of Jno Fentriss her mark is flower deluce ye right ear & ye left a crop wth a nick over itt
Januy 1703/4	Thomas Broock Jun^E his mark is a swallow fork ye left ear crop & hole & over keel ye right
1704	
7^{bE} 20th	Edward Brusbank mark is a croop in each ear & two slitts in each croop
3rd 1704	Wm Davis mark is swall fork & hole in ye right & croop & slitt in ye left eare
4th D^o	Edw: Leam^t: Jun^E mark is croop slitt & under keel ye left swallow fork & under keell ye right
D^o	Jno Leam^t mark is croop slitt & over keel ye right swallow fork & under keell ye left
1704 4th 10^{ber}	Walter Jones mark is under keel & slit in ye right eare
D^o	Alice Jones daughter to ye said Walter mark is under keel ye right eare & a nick in ye left eare
4th July 1705	Jno Sunmoiror mark is a hole in ye right ear & croop & slitt in ye left
(torn)ly 12th 05	Thomas Carraway the right ear crop and slope & a slitt the left ear cropp and slope

	William Carraway son of John Carraway Jun^{E} his mark is the left ear crop and und^{r} sloope & slitt the right ear crop and und^{E} sloope
July ye 12th 1705	Alex^{r} Maclean his mark is a crop slitt and und^{E} sloope in right ear & crop slitt & und^{E} sloope in ye left ear
August	Henry Meremount Sen^{E} mark is slitt in each eare & two nicks und^{E} ye right & one und^{E} ye left

Page 3

Novemb 14th 1705	James Gittery ye son of James Gittery mark is swallo fork ye left ear and a slitt in the right
30th of Aprill 1706	Jno Leamont mark is croop & slitt ye right ear & croop & ye left ear & over keel & under keel
18th Feb^{E}y 1706/7	Geo Moseleys mark is cropp & under keel ye left ear
10th April 1707	Richard Drought Jun^{E} his mark is cropp slitt & nick under ye left ear
	Caleb Drought son of Richard Drought mark is swallow fork & nick under ye left ear & hole in ye right ear of wch mark he hath a cow & yearling wch his father hath given him & all the increase male & female
18th July 1707	Ann Drought her mark is swallow fork & over keel ye right ear & a hole in ye left ear
17th August	Eliz^{E} Keeling daughter to Alex^{E} Keeling mark is slitt & under keel ye right & under keel ye left ear
	Ann Keeling daughter to Idem her mark is over keel ye right & slitt & under keel ye left ear
21st August	Joseph Purvines mark is croop right ear & piece taken out from under ye same & over his old ye left ear
20th 7^{bE} 1707	Thomas Bence mark swallow fork & under keel ye left ear
22^{d}	Jabiss Caswell mark is slitt in ye right ear croop three slitt ye left eare
1707/8 Jan^{E} 17th	Patience Whites mark is swallow fork & under keel in ye right ear
8th Ditto	Edward Carraway son of Jno Carraway Jun^{E} mark swallow fork left ear und^{E} sloop & cropp ye right
23^{d} Jan^{E}y 1707/8	Adam Dollars mark is under keel and over keel ye right ear and half croop under ye left ear being given to him with a heifer yearling by his good father Wm Goddacre
March 1707	Henry Woodhouse Jun^{E} son of Capt Henry Woodhouse mark swallow fork on ye left ear und^{E} keel & over half croop on ye right ear
	Henry Woodhouse mark slitt ye right ear & croop and saw tooth und^{E} ye left ear
	M^{E} Wm Allegood mark croop slitt under and over keel ye left ear
May 4th 1708	Mary Purvine daughter of Lewis Purvine her mark is cropp in ye left & a piece taken out under ye same ear & over keel in ye right ear
6th May 1708	Solomon Waterman mark cropp & slitt ye right ear & over half croop & hole in ye left ear

4th 7bE 1708	Robt Fountaine records is mark to his son Roger being undE keel both ears & nick undE right ear & another over ye left wch mark he saith he have had this forty year
First of DecmbE 1708	Henry Snayle JunE his mark is a half moon taken from under ye left ear & right ear is hole
28 May 1709	Samuell Fentress son of Wm Fentriss his mark is half croop over ye right ear & croop & under keel ye left
28 May 1709	Charles Fentress son of Moses Fentress his mark is swallow fork & flower deluce both
2d June 1709	John Olivers mark croop & slitt ye right ear & a nick cut under ye left ear
20th August	George Simmons son of Henry Simmons his mark is cropp & two slitts right ear & a hole slitt out & under keel ye left
August 31st	Geo Weblin his mark is cropp and hole in the right ear a swallow & a nick undE it the left
	James Williamsons mark crop boath eares over keel & undE keel in the right ear
5th 7bE 1709	Thomas Ryly son of Edw Ryly mark is croop & under keel boath ears & slitt in ye right
Do	Edward Reylays mark swallow fork boath ears & nick under ye right ear
FebEy ye 25th 1709	Robert Bell records for him self ye following mark croop & slitt in ye right ear & over slitt & under slitt in ye left ear
March 18th	ME John Woodhouse SenE mark is swallow fork & under keel ye right ear & half crop over & under keel
May ye 2d 1710	Wm Smith JunE son of Wm Smith marke is flower deluce ye left ear & croop & under keel ye right
July ye 3rd 1710	Job Paskine(?) mark is crop & slitt the left ear
August ye 7th	David Leggatts mark is croop in ye right ear & slitt in ye left ear
9bE 1710	James More mark swallow fork ye left ear & over keell ye right ear & a slitt in ye same
9bE 1710	Robt Richmond mark is croop & half croop under ye right ear & croop slitt & under keel ye left
19th JanEy 1710	Wm Cockrufts mark is croop a hole left ear & nick over it & under keel & over keel ye right

Page 4

February 13	Moriss Fitzgearld mark is swallow fork & under keel ye right ear & croop ye left ear
March ye 18th 1711	Francis Lands mark is croop & under keel ye right & under keel ye left ear
June ye 15th	ME Thomas Walkes mark swallow fork ye left ear & slitt in ye right
July ye 17th	Thomas Harrisons mark croop & slitt ye right ear
Do	James Harrison son of Thomas Harrison mark croop & two slitt ye right ear
July 19th	Henry Holmes mark is croop in left ear & two slitts in it under keel ye right ear & one slitt in ye ear wch mark he have had eighteen yeares last
September 19th	ME Anthony Walke mark is swallow fork ye right ear & hole in ye left for Eastern Branch plantation only

	ME Anthony Walke mark at ye Back Bay is swallow fork ye left ear & half croop under ye right ear
JanEy 26th	ME Henry Moors mark is croop slitt & under keel ye right ear & croop in ye left ear
	ME Henry Moor also another mark under keel & under half croop ye left ear & under half croop ye right
March 6th 1711	Thomas Lovitts mark is croop & two slitts & under keel for ye right ear & flower de luce for ye left ear
	Amy Lovitt daughter of Jno Lovitt mark is croop ye right ear & flower deluce ye left
	Adam Lovitts mark is croop & two slitts ye right ear & flower deluce & slitt ye left
24th May 1710	Cason Moor JunE son of Cason Moor his mark is swallow fork & under keel ye right ear & under keel & over keel ye left ear
1st August 1712	James Leggats mark is croop & under keel of ye left ear & slitt of ye right
NovembE 17th 1712	Henry Moor son of Henry Moor his mark is croop & slitt in ye right ear & with an under nick & half saw tooth over ye left
First day DecembE	James Leamount mark is over keel & slitt in ye right ear & under keel in ye left
8th DecembE	at ye request of ME Lewis Conner ye mark of ME John Fulcher decd being croop & under keel ye right ear ye (left being all whole) is admitted to record
11th March 1712	ME George Pool mark (at Andrews Ground) is croop & two slitts & bitt taken out under ye left ear & half croop over ye right & a bitt taken out under it
21st Aprill 1713	John Hancock son of George Hancock Carpenter his mark recorded by his father is croop & half croop on ye under side in ye right ear
Do	George Hancock Carpenter mark is under keel & slitt ye right ear & under keel ye left
May ye 22d	James Langly mark is croop & left ear & over keel & slitt ye right
28th	ME ChristoE Borroughs his mark is flower deluce ye right ear & croop & half croop under ye left
17th August	ME John Ivy's mark is croop ye right ear & slitt & under keel ye left & ye dew flap cut
7be ye 17th	Me Thomas Ewells mark is croop & under & over keel ye right ear & under keel ye left ear
24th xbE 1713	ME Thomas Attwood mark is croop & half croop under ye right & over ye left ear
23rd JanEy	Thomas Ceaton mark swallow fork in ye right ear & croop & over keel in ye left
Do	Moses Ceaton mark swallow fork ye right & croop ye left ear
Do	Sarah Ceaton mark is swallow fork & under keel ye right ear & croop & slit ye left
Do	Wm Ceaton mark is swallow fork & over keel ye right ear & croop & slitt ye left
Do	James Ceaton mark is swallow fork ye right ear & croop slit & under keel ye left
March ye 6th	Wm Griffens mark (being formerly his sayth recorded for his father) is croop & two slitts in ye cropp in each ear
6th	Alexander Mcclenahan his mark is croop & two slitts in ye croop ye right ear & croop slit & under keel ye left

7th March	Henry Leamounts cattle is marked swallow fork in each ear
Aprill 1714	John Lovit son of John Lovit mark is croop & flower deluce ye right ear & large under keel ye left ear
	John Grinto mark is croop & three slits on ye right ear & a hole in ye left
8th	Wm Richmonds mark is croop & two slits & under keel ye right ear & slit under keel ye left
21st March	MEE Margret Johnson's mark croop & slit ye left ear & over keel & slit in ye right ear
21st March	ME Tully Smyth mark is croop & slitt in ye right ear & saw tooth over ye left

Page 5

Jun 1st 1715	Josiah Morris mark is croop & under keel ye right ear & flower de luce ye left ear
	Wm Morris mark is flower deluce ye right & croop & half croop under ye left ear
21st November	ElizE Fentress mark is croop & flower deluce ye right ear & swallow fork & nick under ye left
28th November	Thomas Owen's mark is croop in each ear
20th xbE 1715	Wm Consalvos mark is croop & three slits in ye right ear
	Wm Consalvos JunE his mark is croop & trees slitts in ye croop both ears
31st xbE	John Busky mark is croop & three slits ye left & swallow fork ye right ear
	Moses Busky mark is swallow fork ye right ear & crop ye left
11th JanEy	Swallow fork & under keel ye right ear & croop & ye slits over ye right ear is Henry Simmons mark
	Richard Simmons son of Henry Simmons his mark is crop & slit ye right ear & under keel & over keel same ear
4th FebEy 1715	Adam Keelings mark is croop & slitt ye right ear & croop & nick under ye left
	John Ryley son of Thomas Ryley mark is swallow fork in each ear under keel ye right & over keel ye left
8th March	Amoss Moseley mark is swallow fork ye left ear & croop ye right ear
Decembr 28th 1716	Samuel Brock's mark is crop & under keel ye left ear & a hole in the right ear
May 22d 1717	Francis Woodhouse mark is crop & ye left ear & three slitts & over half crop ye right ear
Jun 14th 1717	Luke Moseley's mark is swallow fork ye left ear & flower deluse & crop ye right ear
August 16th	William Fentris ye son of William Fentris his mark is slit the right ear & half crop ye upper side of the left eare
Novr 30th:	James Ancell his mark is flower deluse ye right ear & slit & under nick ye left year
Decemr 12th	William Elligood junr his mark is crop slit under & over keel ye right ear & the left ear entirely whole

Feb^{Ey} 5th	George Montgomary his marke is crop and over keel the right eare and a hole in ye left eare
March 3^{d}	John Thorowgood ye son of Mr Argall Thorowgood his mark is crop ye right ear and over keel & under saw tooth ye left eare
March 17th	Robert Huggins ye son of Phillip Huggins his mark is slit the right ear & half ye under part of the left ear
April 13th 1718	Adam Broughton Senr his mark is crop and two slits in each ear & a nick in ye right eare
May 3^{d}	Mr Adam Thorowgood's mark is crop hole & slit in ye right ear & under keel ye left ear
July 19th	Robert Murden's mark is swallow fork ye left ear & crop & under keel ye right eare
Nov^{E} 12th	Batson Whitehurst his mark is swallo fork & under keel ye right ear & under keel ye left ear
	His daughter Mary's mark is swallo fork & a nick under & over ye right ear & under keel ye left
Nov^{E} 12th	John Fentris his mark is flower deluse ye right ear swallo fork & nick under ye left ear
	His son Moses's mark is flower deluse ye right ear swallo fork & nick under & over ye left
Novr 17th	Elizabeth Brinson daughter of John Brinson Senr her mark swallow fork & under keel the right ear and a hole in the left
Decr 9th	Lawrence Bridgers mark is crop & flower deluse ye right ear ye left intirly whole
Xber 9	William Butlers mark is crop under & over keel & slit ye right ear & under keel ye left
Feb^{Ey} 16	Thomas Snailes mark is crop slit & under keel ye left ear & over keel ye right car

Page 6

Feb^{Ey} 18	Daniel Frizell's son Danl: mark is swallo fork & under keel ye left ear & under keel the right eare
	His son Arthurs mark is slit & under keel ye right ear & crop ye left
	His son Francis's mark is slit & under keel ye right eare & crop & slit ye left ear
21st	His daughter Ruths mark is crop & slit ye left ear & under keel ye right eare
Feb^{Ey} 23rd	Samuel Wiles son of Thos: Wiles his mark is crop & half crop ye right eare
	Thos: Wiles Junr his mark is crop & half crop ye left eare ye right intirly whole
	Lemuel Wiles his mark is crop & half crop ye left eare ye right ear under keel
Mar 11th 1718	James Whitehurst Junr his mark is two swallo forks in ye right eare
June 1st 1719	Elizabeth M^{c}gravey daughter of Owen M^{c}gravey dec^{d}: her mark is crop flower deluce & three slits ye left eare crop flower deluce & two slits in ye right eare
Dec^{E} 23^{d} 1719	Mary Lovet daughter of Jno Lovet her mark is swallow fork & flower deluce the right eare under half crop the left eare
Xber 23^{d}	John Buskey's mark swallo fork the right ear & crop & und^{E} & over keel ye left

Xber 23d	Mr. Francis Lands mark is crop & under keel the left ear & under keel the right
Mar 3d 1719	James Fentris son of Jno Fentris his mark swallow fork ye left ear flower deluce ye right
Mar 14th	Horatio son of Capt Hora: Woodhouse mark cropp & slit ye left ear half crop over the right under keele & slit ye same
Mar 26th 1720	Idem mark cropp and two slits the right ear under keel & half crop the left
Aprl 6th 1720	Sarah daughter of Geo: Booth her mark crop & under keele ye right flower deluce & slit ye right
May 28th 1720	Andrew Peacocks mark is crop & two slits ye right & crop & two slits ye left eare
July 6th	Mr Richard Corbets mark is crop the right ear only
(?) 7th 1720	Cornelious Jones his mark is cropp & two slits ye left ear & crop & one slit ye right ear
(?) 5th 1720	John Smith in ye woods his mark flower deluce ye right & crop & flower deluce ye left ear
Decemr 7th	Absalom ye son of James Fentris his mark is cropp & half crop ye under side of ye left ear & two nicks the under side of ye right ear
Augt	Bartholomew Williamson mark is crop ye right ear crop & under sloap the left ear
(?) 4th 1720	James Fentris his mark is swallo fork slit & nick the under side of ye left & flower deluce ye right
(?) 4th 1720	Geo: Wmsons mark is crop slit & a nick under ye right crop & under sloap ye left ear
(?) 11th 1720	James Langley's mark is crop & slit ye left ear & over keel ye right eare
(?) 11th 1720	Joseph Smith's mark is crop & two slits the right ear & crop the left ear
(?) 28th 1720	Robert Dudley Junr his mark is crop ye left & saw tooth ye under side of the right ear
(?) 1st 1720	Stephen Pew's mark is crop slit & under nick ye right crop & two slits the left ear
(?) 8th 1721	William Weblin's mark is crop & half crop ye under side of ye left ear & slit ye right
Idem	William son of ye sd Wm mark crop & half crop ye under side of ye right ear & slit ye left
Idem	George son of ye sd Wm mark swallow fork the left ear crop & over keel ye right
(?) 7th 1721	Aron Fentris mark is crop & half crop ye under side of ye right ear crop & knotch ye under side of the left eare
(?)gt 2d 1721	William ye son of Renatus Land his mark is crop & a knotch ye under side of the right ear under keel & slit ye left ear
Idem	Mary daughter of ye said Renatus her mark crop & knotch under the left ear under keel ye right ear
Idem	Edward son of ye said Renatus his mark cropp & three slits ye left ear under & over keel the right ear

Page 7

JanEy 9th 1721	Thomas Norris's mark is crop & three slits ye left ear & slit the right ear

Idem 10th	John Ackis Junr his mark crop & three slits ye left ear crop slit & under keel ye right
Idem	George Bush's mark crop & three slits ye right ear crop hole & under keel ye left
Idem ye 15	Anthony Moseley planter his mark swallo fork ye left ear crop & two slits ye right
Idem ye 17	William Consalvo Junr his mark is crop & three slits the left ear
Feb^{Ey} 7th 1721	Thomas Brinson his mark is crop and nick under ye right ear
	Idems mark crop and nick under the left eare
Idem ye 10th	Michael Fentris mark nick under & over ye right ear half crop the under side of the left ear
Aprill 4th 1722	Thomas Cartwrights mark is under & over keel ye right ear crop slit & nick under ye left ear
Idem	Frances Cartwrights mark is under & over keel ye right ear crop two slits & nick under ye left ear
Aprill 12th 1722	Robert Masons mark is crop under & over keel ye left ear crop & slit the right ear
Idem	Henry Lovet son of Jno Lovet his mark is crop & two slits ye left ear & flower deluce ye right
May 11th 1722	Mr Christopher Burrowgh's mark is flower deluce ye right ear & crop ye left ear
Sepr 13th 1722	Griffen Floyd's mark is crop & over keel ye right eare crop & hole ye left eare
October 10th 1722	Joseph White's mark is crop & flower deluce ye right ear & under keel the left ear
Idem	William Sutten White's mark is flower deluce ye right ear & under keel the left ear
Nov^{E} 20th 1722	William Seneca's mark is crop & slit the right ear & crop & slit the left ear
Nov^{E} 20th 1722	Thomas Fentris mark crop under & over keel ye right ear crop under & over keel ye left
Decr 5th 1722	Mr George Smyths mark is swallow fork ye right ear & saw tooth over ye left ear
	His son Tully Robinson Smyth's mark crop the right ear saw tooth under the left
Jan^{Ey} 2^{d} 1722	John Mallbone mark swallo fork & under keel ye right ear crop over & under keel ye left
	His son Peter Mallbone mark crop & under keel the right ear & slit ye left ear
Feb^{Ey} 6th 1722	Thomas Elks mark is cropp and under keel the right ear & under keel ye left
Idem 27th 1722	John Morris / head river / mark crop & half crop ye under side of ye right ear & over keel the left eare
March 21st 1722	John Snaile's mark crop nick under the left ear & nick under ye right ear
April 11th 1723	James Mason's mark crop & slit ye right ear & crop & slit the right eare
Idem	John Mundens mark crop ye right ear crop & under half crop ye left ear
July 3rd 1723	John Murray Senr his mark crop & two slits ye left ear and slit the right eare
Idem	Caleb Murray his mark crop & one slit ye left ear & slit the right eare
Augt 7th 1723	Lemuel James mark is under & over keel ye right ear swallo fork & under keel ye left
Idem	Margret Williams her mark crop & half crop the right and left ears
Idem	Elizabeth Williams her mark crop & two slits in ye right and left ears

Idem	John Williams his mark swallow fork & under keel ye right & left ears
Idem	Mary daughter of Edw: James her mark crop & hole ye right crop hole and under keel ye left ear
Augt 13th 1723	Mr Richard Cheshire's mark crop & two slits the left ear & under keel the right ear
Sepr 2^{d} 1723	William Keeling's mark crop slit & under keel ye right ear under keel & over sloap ye left
Idem	His son William's mark crop slit & under keel ye right ear under keel & over sloap ye left
Sepr 21st 1723	Mr James Nimmo his mark is crop & ye left ear, being ye mark of his wifes father and grandfather Jacob Johnson ye Elder & younger

Page 8

Octob 2^{d} 1723	Lemuel Hargrove his mark is crop the left ear and slit the right ear
Octo^{r} 3 1723	Reodolphus Mallbone his mark is over sloap and under keel ye right ear
Idem	His son Charles Mallbone's mark is over sloap under keel the left ear
Idem	James Allbritton his mark is crop & hole in ye right ear swallo fork & under keel ye left ear
Idem	John Rutland his mark crop slit & under keel ye right ear slit & under keel ye left ear
Idem	Thomas Cotance his mark is swallow fork ye left ear crop two slits & under keel ye right
8ber 26th 1723	Reodolphus Mallbone son of Peter Malbone his mark is swallo fork the right & left ears and slit and nick under ye right ear
Sepr 2^{d} 1724	James Heath's mark crop & under keel the right ear slit & under keel the left ear
Decem 15th 1724	Mr Thomas Haynes his mark over sloap & under keel ye right ear & over sloap ye left ear
Idem	His daughter Frances mark over sloap & under keel ye left ear & over sloap ye right ear
Feby 6 1724	John Flanagan's mark crop two slits & nick under ye right ear & over & under keel ye left
Idem 7th	John M^{c}clanhan Junr: mark half crop ye under side of ye right ear & under keel the left ear
Novr 27 1724	Peter Floyds mark is crop slit & under keel ye right ear over keel & slit the left eare
Decr 2^{d} 1724	John Key black smith his mark is three slits in ye right & three slits in ye left ears
Jan^{Ey} 4th 1724	Reodolphus Malbone (son of Peter) his mark swallow fork the right and left ears and slit & nick under the left ear
January 30th 1724	Thomas Albritton's mark crop and staple the right ear and crop the left ear
March 2^{d} 1724	Henry Snaile his mark cropp and under half cropp the left ear
March 3^{d} 1724	Simon Whitehurst his mark is cropp and under keel the right ear
Aprill 12th 1725	John Shipp his mark is swallow fork & hole in ye right ear & swallow fork and a hole in ye left ear
May 5th 1725	William Moseley (son of Luke) his mark swallow fork ye right ear crop & flower deluce ye left ear
October 13th 1725	David Holt Junr his mark crop & two slits in ye right ear under keel & hole in the left ear

July 5th 1725	James Kempe his mark under keel ye left ear crop & flower deluce the right ear
Idem	Walter Vowels his mark crop under keel & hole in ye right ear crop under keel & slit in ye left ear
July 7th 1725	Isabella Lovett (daughter of John) her mark swallow fork & flower deluce ye left ear and under half cropp the right ear
August 23^{d} 1725	Dinah Jones wid^{o} her mark is crop & slit in ye right ear & over keel on ye left ear
(?) ye 10th 1725	William Creedle his mark swallow fork & under keel the right ear & slit the left ear
(?)^{Ey} 27th 1725	John James son of John James Senr his mark is over & under keel ye right ear & under & over keel & slit the left eare
Idem	The said James his son Guisborn's mark is under & over keel & a hole in ye right ear & under & over keel & a slit in ye left ear
Idem	His son Thomas James his mark crop hole & nick under ye right ear crop & hole in ye left ear
(?)b^{Ey} ye 2^{d} 1725	James Cason Junr his mark is crop & half crop ye right ear slit & under keel the left ear
(?) 19th 1725	Mr Thomas Lawson his mark is crop the right eare & slit the left eare
March 21st 1725	James (son of James) Fentris his mark is swallow fork & slit ye left eare, & flower deluce ye right
April 16th 1726	John James son of Edward James his mark swallow fork the left & crop the right ear
	His son John James his mark is under & over keel the right and left ears
(?)y 4th 1726	Henry James his mark is under & over keel the left eare, and over keel the right ear
Idem	Robert James his mark is under & over keel ye right & over keel & under half crop ye left
Idem	Charles Henly his mark is crop & hole the right eare & crop & under keel the left eare

Page 9

May 4th 1726	Batson Whitehurst Junr his mark is swallow fork the right eare & over keel ye left eare
Idem	Mary Simmons daughter Malbone Simmons her mark is under keel & slit ye left ear & slit ye right eare
August 3^{d} 1726	Thomas Old his mark is crop the right eare & crop and under nick the left eare
October 5th 1726	Edward Bonney his mark is crop & two slits ye left ear crop slit under & over keel ye right ear
Idem	Florence Sullivant his mark crop and slit the left ear and slit the right eare
Idem	Job Taynor his mark is crop under keel the right ear and slit the left eare
Idem	George Norris his mark is crop & two slits ye left ear slit & nick under ye right ear
Novr 10th 1726	John Lovet (son of Lancaster) his mark crop slit & over keel ye right flower deluce ye left ear
Idem	William (son of ye said Lancaster) his mark crop & over keel ye right ear flower deluce ye left ear

Decemb^{r} 3^{d} 1726	Henry Woodhouse (son of Francis) his mark crop & three slits ye right eare over half crop ye left
Idem	John Ward his mark crop & saw tooth ye under side of ye left & swallow fork ye right eare
Decemb^{r} 10th 1726	John Cartwright Senr his mark crop slit & flower deluce ye left under & over keel ye right ear
Idem	William James Junr his mark crop the left ear & swallow fork the right eare
Idem	Henry (son of Henry) Woodhouse his mark swallow fork ye right ear under keel & over sloap ye left
Jan^{Ey} 21st 1726	Thomas Hartly his mark crop & half crop ye under side of ye right ear & slit ye left year
Idem	John Murden Junr his mark is crop the left eare and nick under ye right eare
Idem	Simon Whitehurst his mark crop & under keel ye right ear & saw tooth ye under side of ye left ear
Idem	John Willbur Junr his mark is crop & over half crop the left ear & slit ye right eare
Jan^{Ey} 26 1726	Cason Moore (son of Thomas) his mark under keel & over sloap ye right & under keel & over sloap the left ears
Feb^{Ey} 2^{d} 1726	Elizabeth White daughter of William White her mark crop & under keel ye right & crop& under keel the left ears
Feb^{Ey} 20th 1726	Lewis Bakers mark is swallo fork the right ear and flower deluce the left ear
April 4th 1727	Thomas Franklins mark is swallow fork & under keel ye right ear crop slit & under keel the left ear
Idem	Daniel Franklin's mark is swallo fork ye right ear crop & under nick ye left ear
May 5th 1727	John Griffen Junr his mark is crop & hole in the right ear ye left intirly whole
Idem	Ann Cooper gives unto her daughter Lidia Cooper two young cows & calves marked follows under keel ye right ear crop nick over & slit in ye left ear
May 22^{d} 1727	Robert Whitehurst his mark swallo fork under keel & a hole in the right ear swallo fork and under keel the left ear
Idem 23^{d}	James Wilbur his mark crop & over half crop ye left ear slit & over keel ye right ear
July 5th 1727	James (son of Thomas) Cason his mark slit & under keel ye right ear & slit ye left ear
Idem 28th	Daniel Frizels mark swallo fork the right ear under keel & a hole in the left ear
Idem	His son John Frizels mark is under keel & slit ye right ear crop & half crop the under side of ye left ear
Idem	His son Edward Frizels mark is slit & under keel ye right ear swallo fork the left ear
Idem	Renaltus Land his mark is crop the right ear & under keel the left ear look order book august 1729 & record book folio 330 new
Idem	His son John Lands mark two swallo forks in ye right ear over sloap & under keel y^{e} (torn)
August 3st 1727	Thomas (son of Thomas) Cason his mark crop & hole in ye left ear & three nicks under right ear
Idem	Bartholomew Bond his mark crop & under keel the left ear & crop ye right ear

Idem ye 5th	Aron (son of Moses) Fentris his mark swallo fork and a nick under the left ear
Idem	Solomon (son of said Moses) Fentris his mark is swallo fork & nick under & over the left ear
Idem	Lemuel (son of ye said Moses) Fentris his mark is swallow fork & a nick over ye left ear
	It is ye desire of ye said Moses that if either of these three son die without lawful issue then this mark to desend to his brother Hezekiah Fentris

Page 10

September 4th 1727	William Bonney Senr: his mark is crop & nick under ye right ear; & crop & nick u under ye left ear
Idem	Richard Bonney his mark is crop & a nick under ye left ear; & over keel ye right ear
Idem	William Bonney Junr: his mark is crop & nick under ye right ear; & over keel ye right ear
Idem ye 6th 1727	John Williams his mark is crop and over keel the left ear; and a hole in the right eare
October 4th	Amy daughter of William Keeling her mark under keel & slit ye right ear: swallow fork ye left ear
Idem 19th	John Williams Senr: his mark swallo fork ye left ear: two nicks over & one nick under ye right ear
Idem	Josiah Morris Junr: his mark crop & under keel ye left ear: flower deluce the right ear
Novr 30th 1727	George Williamson his mark crop & slit the right ear: crop & under sloap the left ear
Idem	John (son of John) Fentris his mark swallo fork & nick under ye left ear: one nick over & two nicks under the right ear
Idem	Aron Suggs his mark swallo fork ye right ear saw tooth ye underside slit & nick over ye left ear
Decr 29 1727	John Consaul his mark crop the right ear, under keel & slit the left ear
JanEy 3rd 1727	James Morris his mark half crop ye underside of ye right ear; flower deluce ye left ear
Idem	William Morris Junr his mark slit & under keel the right ear swallo fork & under keel ye left
JanEy 9th 1727	Edward Sharp his mark over half crop ye right ear & slit the left ear
Idem 19	Sarah Woodhouse her mark swallo fork the right ear under half crop the left ear
Idem	Jonathan Woodhouse his mark under keel & over half ye left ear slit 7 under keel ye right
April 3rd 1728	Ruth James her mark swallo fork the right ear and nick under the left eare
Idem	Sarah James her mark is swallo fork the left ear, & a nick under the right ear
Idem	Mary (daughter of William) Gornto her mark crop & three slits ye left ear, under keel and over half crop the right ear
Idem	Margret Gornto her mark crop three slits & nick under ye left ear, & one nick under ye right
May 1st 1728	Thomas (son of William) Morris his mark is under keel & over keel ye right, & left ears

May 16 1728	Joh Williams Junr his mark is crop & slit the right ear, hole & under keel the left ear
D^{o}: 25th 1728	James Gittery his mark is crop two slits and under keel the right ear
June 5th 1728	Edwar^{d} (son of John James Junr) his mark is crop ye right ear & crop the left ear
July 23^{d} 1728	Francis Moseley Junr his mark is crop & over keel the left ear, & under keel the right ear
August 7th 1728	Francis Land Junr his mark swallo fork under keel & over keel the left year, & crop the right ear
Idem	His son Johns mark crop and over keel the right ear, and under keel the right eare
Idem	Richard Land his mark is crop slit and keel the right ear, & crop & under keel the left ear
(torn)temb^{r} 4th 1728	Adam Ackis his mark is under keel & over keel the left ear, and swallow fork ye right ear
Idem	William Cox his mark is over sloap and under keel ye right ear; & hole in the left ear
(illegible) 5th 1728	Amy Lovett her mark is crop & over keel the left ear: & flower deluce the right ear
(torn) 22^{d} 1728	Anthony Wiles his mark is over half crop the right ear, & over half crop the left ears
(torn) 18th 1728	John Norris his mark is crop and under half crop the left ear; & flower deluce ye right eare
Idem	William Harvey his mark is crop slit & over keel the right ear, & crop & over keel the left
(torn)^{Ey} 18th 1728/9	Joseph Otterson his mark is swallow fork over keel & under keel ye right and left ears
(torn)ay 12th 1730	George Wishard his mark is crop & slit ye left ear & under & over keel ye right ear
(torn)^{Ey} 14th 1729	Nowdinah Dauge her mark is crop & three slits the right ear, and a nick under the left ear
(torn)^{Ey} 27th 1729	Thomas Moore son of Capt Henry Moore his mark swallow fork the right ear, over keel and slit under the left ear
Idem	William Moore / son of ye said Henry / his mark swallow fork & under & over keel the left ear, & under & over keel the right ear
Idem	Cason Moore / son of ye said Henry / his mark, swallow fork the left ear, over keel & slit under the right ear

Page 11

March 30th 1730	Robert Dudley Senr his mark is crop the right ear, under & over keel the right ear
Aprill 1st 1730	Henry Consaul his mark is crop & slit the left ear nick under the right ear, given him as his father says by Richard Gardner who marryed with Elizabeth the daughter of Ad: keeling dec^{d}:
Aprill 27 1730	James Leamount his mark crop & slit ye right ear over keel & nick under ye left ear
July first 1730	Andrew Nicklis his mark is crop the right ear; crop & half crop ye under side of the left ear
July 18th 1730	John Salmon (the son of John) his mark swallow fork notch over & under ye right ear saw tooth ye under side of the left ear & a small piece taken of ye upper side thereof
July 21st 1730	William Broughton his mark is crop ye left ear, crop & half crop ye under side of ye right ear

August 19th 1730	Thomas Wishard his mark is under keel ye right ear, swallow fork & slit the left ear
Septembr 25th 1730	Henry Whitehurst his mark is swallo fork & nick under ye right ear, swallo fork & nick under and over the left ear
Octobr 29 1730	Francis Ackis his mark is crop and three slits the right ear crop & one slit ye left ear
January 5th 1730	Frances Condon her mark is swallo fork & under keel ye right ear, under half crop ye left ear
January 21st 1730	John Nicklis Junr his mark is crop & half crop ye upper side of the right ear, crop & half crop the upper side of the left ear
Idem	Mr William Spiring his mark is swallo fork the right ear & a slit in the left ear
JanEy 22d 1730	Richard Smith his mark is swallow fork the right ear, & swallo fork the left ear
Idem	John Edwards his mark is swallo fork & un keel ye left ear crop under & over keel ye right ear
FebEy 10th 1730	Mr John Connyer's mark is crop slit & under keel ye right ear and under keel in the left ear
March 15th 1730	James son of Jno Smith his mark is flower deluce & crop ye right ear & swallo fork ye left ear
Idem	James / son of Thos / Lovett his mark is crop slitt and over keel the right ear ye left intirely hole
FebEy 27 1730	Jane Gornto her mark is crop & three slits in ye left ear & under keel ye right eare
Idem	Thomas Haynes / son of John / his mark is crop slit & under half crop the right ear & under keel & over sloap the left ear
Idem	John Gornto Junr his mark is crop and hole in ye right ear, over half crop ye left ear
Mar ye 15 1730	Samuel Tatem his mark is crop & two slits the left ear, and two slits in the right ear
Idem	John Turner his mark is crop & two slits the right ear, and two slits in the left ear
Aprill 2d 1731	Joyce Thelaball her mark is crop & swallow fork ye right ear, & under & over keel ye left
April 7th 1731	Ann Nicklis her mark is crop half crop ye upper side of the left ear and under keel the same crop & half crop ye upper side & under keel the right ear
May 6 1731	Lancaster Lovett / son of Lancaster / his mark is crop slit over keel ye left ear, flower deluce ye right
August 4 1731	Lemuel Langley his mark swallow fork & under keel ye right ear, over & under keel ye left ear
August 25 1731	William Edmonds his mark is swallow fork the left ear, & nick over the right ear
Sepr 1 1731	John Brown / son of Edward / his mark is crop the left ear, and slit the right ear
Idem	Thomas Gardner his mark is cropp and a hole in the right ear, and a hole in the left ear
October 30th 1731	William Hancock his mark crop & under keel the left ear, slit and over keel the right ear
NovembE 25 1731	John Hunter his mark is crop and under keel the right ear & saw tooth under the left ear
DecembE 8th 1731	Thomas Spratt Junr his mark crop under keel & a hole in ye right ear crop & slit the left ear

Idem 21st 1731	Mary Gardner her mark is crop the left ear & nick under the right ear
March 1st 1731	John / son of John / Smith his mark is cropp and over keel the left ear
Idem	John Scott his mark is crop and over keel the left ear, and a hole in the right ear
March 10th 1731	William Martin his mark is cropp and slit the left ear
Feb^{Ey} 9th 1732	Wm Bonny son of John Bonny his mark is crop boath ears & a nick under boath ears, his father Richd Bonny assigns all his right & title to ye said mark
March 7th 1733/4	Simon Whitehurst Junr son of Simon Whitehurst Senr his mark is crop & over keel the right ear and the left intirely whole

Page 12

April 5th 1732	Jacob Langley his mark is swallow fork ye right ear crop & under half crop the left ear being the mark he bought with his land
July 31st 1732	Horatio Woodhouse his mark is swallow fork & under keel the left ear, over half crop & under keel the right ear
(torn)ber 6 1732	Sevill Gasking his mark is crop and two slits the left ear
Jun 9 1733	Matthew Kelly his mark is swallow fork & under keel ye right ear, crop & under keel the left ear
July 4th 1733	William Cornick his mark is crop & two slits the left ear & over half crop ye right ear
Idem	His daughter Barbara's mark is crop & two slits ye right ear & over half crop ye left ear
July 14th 1733	John Kelley his mark is crop & a hole in ye left ear, under saw tooth the right ear
Idem	Margret Kelley her mark is crop & nick under ye left ear, & under saw tooth ye right ear
Octob^{E} 4 1733	Henry Matthias his mark is crop & slit the left ear, under keel the right ear
Nov^{E} 8 1733	Maj^{r} Maximilian Boush his mark is crop & slit the right ear, half crop over the left and a round piece underneath taken out of ye same
(torn)ber 4 1733	Sarah Whitehurst her mark is crop & a nick under ye right ear, & slit the left ear
(torn)eb^{Ey} 14 1733	Matthew Pallett his mark is crop ye right ear, under & over keel the left ear
Idem	John Pallett his mark is crop & slit the right ear, under & over keel the left ear
Idem	John Pallett his mark is crop & slit the left ear, under & over keel the right ear
Idem	Smith Shepherd his mark swallo fork & under keel the right ear, & over keel ye left ear
(torn) eb^{Ey} 20th 1733	Titus Cherry his mark is crop & under keel ye right ear, & crop & nick under ye left ear
Mar 6 1733	John Wickings his mark is crop & under keel ye right ear, crop and slit ye left ear
Idem	His daughter Elizabeth Wickings her mark is crop & under keel ye right ear, crop & two slits the left ear
Mar 19 1733	William Fentris / son of John / his mark is swallo fork nick under & over ye left ear, one nick over & two nicks under the right ear

Idem	Lemuel Fentris (son of John) his mark is swallo fork & nick under the left ear, flower deluce the right ear
April 3^{d} 1734	William Buskey his mark is crop & slit the left ear, and crop the right ear
April 3 1734	John Burgess his mark is crop & under half crop ye right ear, & over keel the left ear
May 1st 1734	John Keeling his mark is under keel & over slope ye right ear & slit ye left ear
Idem	Martin Burrass his mark is crop & tow slits ye left ear, & crop the right ear
May 20th 1734	James Langley his mark is over keel the right ear, crop & slit the left ear
D^{o}: 25th	Robert Burrough his mark is crop & two slits ye left ear, flower deluce ye right ear
Jun 13th 1734	Horatio / son of Henry / Woodhouse his mark is crop & slit ye right ear flower deluce and slit the left ear
Jun 27 1734	William Cox Junr his mark is swallo fork ye left ear, over keel the right ear
July 22^{d} 1734	John Shipp Junr his mark is crop the left ear, under keel & slit the right ear
Septemb 7th 1734	Arthur Sayer his mark is under keel ye left & slit the right ear
Decemb 7 1734	Palmer Moseleys mark is swallow fork & over keel & a nick under ye left ear ye right intirely hole
Idem	Jonathan / son of Jno / Saunders Dec^{d} his mark is under keel & a nick on ye upper part of ye right ear and under half crop ye left ear
Decemb^{r} 7 1734	John Scotts mark is crop over keel & nick under ye right ear & a whole in the left ear
Idem	Frances Scotts mark is crop over keel & nick under ye left ear & whole in the right ear
Idem	Richd Cooks mark is over sloop & under keel ye left ear, crop & half crop under ye right ear
Xber 9	John Edmonds mark is swallo fork & under keel ye right ear ye left ear intirely whole

Page 13

FebEy 11 1734	John Tainer's mark is flower deluce each ear
17	Blandinah Thrilwind her mark is slit ye right & left ears
May 7 1735	Francis Gornto her mark is crop & tree slitts ye right ear & crop ye left ear
Idem	John Flear's mark is swallo fork & under keel ye left ear & slit ye right ear
Jun 7	Wm Mackclanhans mark is under half crop ye left ear & under keel ye right ear
July	The mark that was Mary Lovetts is by her father ordered to her sister Betty Lovet
17	Amy Scotts mark is swallo fork & under keel ye right ear & slit ye left ear
Idem	Betty Dale her mark is swallow fork & under keel ye right & left ears
FebEy 26	Wm Dales mark is swallo fork & under keel ye left ear & under keel ye right ear
1736, Aprill 7	Phillip Malbones mark is crop & under keel ye right ear, slit & under keel ye left ear
May 5 1736	Edward Lands mark is crop & over keel ye right ear & over keel ye left ear

8	Arthur (son of W^{m}) Morris his mark is under half crop ye right & left ears
12	John Huggins his mark is crop & hole ye right ear & under keel & hole ye left ear
15	Mr Nathaniel Newton's mark is crop & under half crop ye left ear & under keel ye right ear
Octob^{r} 10	Mr Henry Barlow's mark is crop ye right ear & a diamond & half diamond cut out of ye left ear
	Thos Barlow son of said Henry his mark is crop & slit ye right ear & a diamond & half diamond ye left ear
	Richd Barlow son of s^{d} Henry his mark is crop & two slits ye right ear & a diamond & half diamond cut out of the left ear
	Henry Barlow Junr son of s^{d} Henry his mark is a diamond & half diamond the right ear and crop the left ear
15	Mr George Wisharts mark is swallow fork the left ear
9^{ber} 3rd	John Hopkins Junr his mark is crop slit & under keel ye left ear & under keel ye right ear
Xber 1	John Fentris Senr his mark is crop & slit the right ear ye left & under (unreadable) under keel
14	Persilla Fentriss's mark is crop slit & under keel ye left ear, under & over keel ye right ear
14	John Berry Junr his mark is swallow fork ye right ear crop two slits & (torn) ye left ear
14	William Fentriss Junr his mark is crop a hole & slit ye right ear ye left intirely whole
16	Robert James his mark is crop & half crop ye right ear & swallow fork ye left ear
1737 Jun 11	Jane Otterson her mark is swallow fork & under keel ye right ear & swallow fork & over keel the left ear
D^{o}	Martha Otterson her mark is swallow fork & under keel ye left ear & swallow fork & over keel the right ear
D^{o}	Jonathan James / son of Jno James Senr / his mark is crop both ears & under keel ye right
July 6 1737	Matthew Pallets mark is crop the left ear & under & over keel the right ear
Septr 9 1737	Jno Bray his mark is crop under keel & over keel ye right ear & over keel the left ear
Octob^{r} 5 1737	William Nash his mark is saw tooth ye under side of ye right ear crop & under keel ye left ear
Novemb^{r} 24 1737	Ja^{s} Gainers mark is crop & slit the right ear & crop the left ear
Decemb 5 1737	Eliz^{a} M^{c}cartys mark is swallo fork & nick under the right & left ears
JanEy 10 1737	Henry Snaile his mark is crop & under half crop the right ear
Aprill 1st 1738	Jno Barns Junr his mark is crop & under keel the right & left ears
27	Jno Huggins his mark is under half crop the right ear under keel & a nick on the upper part of the left ear
29	Thomas Hunters mark is under keel ye left ear & saw tooth under ye right ear
29	James Hunters mark is crop & slit ye right ear & saw tooth under ye left ear
May 3rd	Mary Lovet's mark is crop & over keel the left ear flower deluce & slit the right ear

3	Henry Lovets mark is crop over keel & slit the left ear flower deluce & slit the right ear
July 13	Alexandr Fentriss his mark is over half crop the left ear; crop & under sloap the right ear
	Charles Norris his mark is crop slit & under keel the right ear flower deluce the left ear
14	Robt Dearmore his mark is under keel the right ear only
Augst 21	Mr Sal Boush's mark is under keel & over sloap the right ear & under keel the left ear
Ober 5	Anthony Burrough's mark is crop & under half crop ye left ear & flower deluce the right ear

Page 14

Novembr 24	Eliza Lovetts mark is crop & two slitts the left ear flower deluce slit out the right ear
JanEy 3rd	Henry Cornicks mark is crop the left ear, over half crop & slit in the under side thereof the right ear
9	Joel Cornick's mark is crop two slitts & under keel the left ear & over half crop the right ear
FebEy 7	Jas Moore (woods) his mark is crop slitt & over keel the left ear; two nicks under the right
15	Edward Land's mark is under keel the left ear only
1739 Apr 4	Sarah Ashby's mark is crop under & over keel the right ear, under keel & nick over the left ear
4	Moses Fentris the younger's mark is swallow fork & nick over ye right ear, nick under & over ye left ear
12	Thos Langley son of Leml his mark is crop & under half crop the left ear
30	David Scotts mark is crop under & over keel the right ear, crop & under keel the left ear
	Richd Scotts mark is crop under 7 over keel & slit the right ear crop & under keel the left ear
May 2d	Mr Thomas Hunters mark is under keel the right ear & saw tooth under the left ear. This mark is recorded as the right of said Hunter became his the contrary ear to his right mark & he had mark'd some of his (unreadable) soe
3	William Henly his mark is crop & a hole the right ear & crop & three slitts the left ear
July 17	George Williamson Junr his mark is crop & slitt the right ear, crop & under sloap the left ear, which mark his father gave to him in the presence of Jno & Wm Fentriss junr
Augst 7	Robt Roe his mark is swallow fork the left ear crop & under keel the right ear
9	Joshua Land his mark is crop the right ear & a hole in the left ear
Septembr	James Bannister's mark is swallow fork the right ear flower deluce & slit out ye left
25	Henry Keeling mark is under keel & over sloap the left ear & slit out the right ear
Novembr 28	Fra. Wilburs mark is crop & under half crop ye right ear over keel & nick under ye left ear

28	Sa^{l} Wilbur's mark is crop & over half crop ye right ear & slit the left ear
28	William Wilbur jun^{E} his mark is crop & over half crop the left ear, slit and under keel the right ear
DecembE 19	Solomon Sugg's mark swallow fork & nick over the right ear crop & three slitts the left ear
19	John Kempe's mark is crop slit & nick under & over the right ear & under sloap ye left
21	Joel Whitehurst his mark is crop & hole ye right ear & slit the left ear
21	Odian Whitehurst his mark is crop & hole the left ear & slit the right ear
29	James Cotton his mark is crop & nick under the left ear & a hole in the right ear
JanEy 11	Richard Gardner's mark is crop the right ear & nick under the left ear
Mar 1	Francis Malbone's mark is under keel & over sloap ye right ear slit & under keel ye left
8	Lem^{l} Cornick his mark is crop & slit the left ear over half crop the right ear
8	Idems mark is crop & slit the right ear & over half crop the left ear
8	Jno Woodhouse's mark is crop slit & under keel ye right ear & under keel ye left ear
8	Phillip Woodhouse mark is crop & slit the right ear, & over keel the left ear
1740 Aprill 2	Thos son of Ja^{s} Harrison his mark is crop & under sloap the right ear, the left ear whole
May 9	William Jacob his mark is under half crop the left ear, over keel slit the right ear
9	Capt Thos Walkes mark is swallow fork either ear & slit the contrary
June 4	Richd Whitehurst mark is swallow fork ye right ear crop & a hole the left ear
12	Ja^{s} Ashby's mark is swallow fork ye right ear over & under keel the left ear
Augst 7	Mary(?) P(unreadable)e daughter of Thos Langley her mark is crop under half crop & slit in the left ear the right ear whole
Septr 2	Thos Lesters mark is crop & hole the left ear the right intirely whole
October 1	John Sherwood's mark is over keel the right ear, crop & under keel the left ear
Novemb 15	Rich^{d} / son of John Stone / his mark is swallow fork the right ear & flower deluce the left ear
15	Saml Davis his mark is swallow fork & over keel the right ear & flower deluce the left ear

Page 15

1740 9ber 26	Loyd (son of George) Jones his mark is swallow fork the left ear, & saw tooth under the right ear

FebEy 3	John Keeling Sen[r] his mark is crop & two slitts the right ear & over keel & nick under the left ear
3	John son of the above said John Keeling his mark is crop & two slitts the left ear & over keel & nick under the right ear
3	Arthur Sayer his mark is under keel the right ear & slit out the left ear which said mark was his fathers
June (omitted)	Rob[t] Richmond his mark is swallo fork under & over keel the right ear & crop the left ear
March 1739	Francis Snaile her mark is a nick over the right ear crop & under half crop the left ear
(omitted)	Mary Snail her mark is a nick over the right ear crop & under half crop the left ear
	Hillary Snaile his mark is crop under half crop & a nick over the left ear
FebEy 1739	John Senica his mark is crop & two swallow fork the right ear, crop slit and over keel the left
(omitted)	
1741 June	Abraham Willeroy his mark is swallow fork the right & left ear
Aug[st] 3	Batson Whitehurst jun[E] his mark is crop slit & under keel the left ear
Septemb[r] 17	William Wilburs mark is crop & over half crop y[e] right ear and saw tooth under the left ear
	Jn[o] son of William Wilbur his mark is crop & under keel the right ear and crop & over keel the left ear
Decemb[r] 26	Tully Moseley's mark is crop either ear & over half crop the contrary ear
	William Hancock's mark is under keel both ears & slit in the left or right
FebEy 3	Jn[o] (son of Ja[s]) Harrison his mark is crop & under slop the left ear the right intirely whole
10	Edward (son of Maj[r] Fra[s]) Moseley his mark is crop the right ear & under keel the left ear
March 15	Worsell Aldersons mark is crop & hole the right ear & slit over the left ear
D[o]	James Alderson son of d[o] his mark is crop & hole the left ear & slit out the right ear
D[o]	John Alderson son of d[o] his mark is crop the right ear & under half crop the left ear
17	Thomas Grainger's mark is flower deluce each ear
23[d]	Lancaster Lovett Sen[e] his mark is crop & slit the right ear, & flower deluce the left ear
1742 May 5th	Aquilla Munden his mark is crop & under half crop the left ear & crop & two slitts y[e] right
24	James Broughtons mark is crop & slit the left ear crop & over half crop y[e] right
July 7	Enoch Whitehursts' mark is crop & over half crop the left ear & nick over the right ear
7	John Biddle's mark is under keel & slit the right & left ears

16	Charles Hill's mark is crop two slitts & under keel the left ear & under & over keel the right ear
October 20th	Daniel (son of Saml) Fentriss his mark is over square the left ear & slit out the right ear
January 7	Adam Keeling (son of Adam) his mark is crop & slit the left ear over keel & nick under the right ear
	William Keeling (son of d^{o}) his mark is swallow fork & nick under the right ear & a hole in the left ear
26	Richard Nicholas's mark is crop & under keel the right ear crop & over half crop the left ear
	William Bodnam's mark is swallow fork either ear & two slits in the contrary ear
1743 Aprill 27	James Petrees mark is crop & slit the left ear & flower deluce the right ear
Ditto	Edward Sharps mark is under half crop the left ear slit out & nick under (faded out)
	Jeremiah Petrees mark is crop & slit the left ear flower deluce & hole the right ear

Page 16

1743 Jun 1	Thomas Griffens mark is under saw tooth the right ear crop and over keel the left ear
D^{o}	John Cannon mark is slit the right ear and a hole in the left ear
D^{o}	Smith / son of Smith / Shepard his mark is over keel the right ear swallow fork and under keel the left ear
Ober 22	James Fitzgerralds mark is crop & under keel the left ear & a hole in the right ear
FebEy 10	John / son of Titus / Cherry his mark is crop & under keel the left ear the right ear whole
Idem	Mr William Robinson mark is under saw tooth the right & left ears
Idem	James / son of W^{m} / Denny his mark is crop & under keel the right ear & a hole in the left ear
March 2	Jacob / son of James / Moore his mark is crop & slit the right ear & two nick under the left ear
	Ezekiell son of D^{o} his mark is crop slit & over keel the right ear & two nicks under the left ear
17	Thomas Jones shoemaker his mark is swallow fork & a hole the right ear the left whole
1744 Mar	Ezekiell / son of Thos Hill jun^{r} his mark is crop & over keel the right ear & a hole in the left ear
Aprill 16	John Hardens mark is crop & slitt the right ear & crop the left ear

25	Henry / son of Henry / Lamount his mark is swallow fork & under keel the right ear & swallow fork the left
May	Richard Brinsons mark is crop & three slits the left ear & crop & hole the right ear
	John Brinson son of D^{o} his mark is crop & three slits right ear & crop & hole the left ear
September	Tully / son of Charles / Smyth his mark is crop & slit the left ear & saw tooth over the right ear
	Nathaniel McClenahans mark is crop under & over keel the right ear and slit out the left ear or crop over & under keel the left ear & slit out the right
	Idems mark is crop under & over keel the left ear & slitt out the right ear
	Sarah Anne Veal her mark is crop the right ear the left ear intirely hole
	Mr William Robinson his mark is swallow fork the left ear & saw tooth und^{r} the right ear
Novemb^{r} 22	Henry Chapmans mark is under over keel & slit the right ear crop & under keel the left ear
	Frances daughter of the said Henry / Chapman her mark is crop & two slits the right ear and under keel the left ear
Decemb^{r} 19	John / son of John / Harvey his mark is crop & under keel the right ear & under keel the left ear
	Mr Edward Hack Moseleys mark is swallow fork the right ear which mark was his grandfathers
	Mr Edward Hack Moseleys other mark is crop the left ear & under keel the right ear which mark was his fathers
	Capt John Thorowgoods mark is swallow fork the right ear & under keel the left ear
March 15	Capt James Moores mark is crop & under keel the right ear & crop & two slitts the left ear
Mar 28th	William Martins mark crop under keel & hole in the right ear crop under keel & slit in the left ear
Aprill 6	Samuel son of James Moore his mark is crop & under half crop the right ear & a hole and slit out the left ear
D^{o}	Henry Moore son of ditto his mark is crop & under half crop the left ear & a hole & slitt out the right ear
8	Thomas son of Samuel Wiles his mark is swallow fork the right ear & crop & over half crop the left ear
May 14th	Josiah Morris son of Willm Morris his mark is crop the right ear under keel & slit out the left ear
June 4	Francis / daughter of Mary / Smith her mark is crop slit & nick under & over the left ear & flower deluce the right ear

July 1	Eliz^{a} daughter of Thos Langley her mark is crop under half crop & slit the right ear the left entirely whole
August 10th	Luke Moseleys mark swallow fork the right & left ear
26	Charles / son of Fra / Harvey his mark crop & (unreadable) keel the right ear and flower deluce the left ear
	Katherine / daughter of Adam / Ackiss her mark is swallow fork the right ear & under keel & over keel the left ear

Page 17

1745	
JanEy	Edward Davises mark is crop & under keel the right ear crop & a hole in the left ear
28	William James / son of Jno James Senr dec^{d} / his mark is crop the right ear and swallow fork the left ear
February 6	Pat Murphy's mark is swallow fork & over keel the right ear slit and under keel the left ear
March 5	John Salmons mark is swallow fork the right ear two nicks under & one nick over the left ear
19	William (son of Charles) Edwards his mark is crop & flower deluce both ears
1746 Mar 29	Capt Lemuel Langley's mark is swallow fork & under keel the right ear & under & over keel the left ear
Apr 9	Mr William Purdy his mark is crop & two slitts the right ear & crop & under keel the left ear
	Thos Langleys mark is crop the right ear the left ear intirely whole
30	Saml Nicholas (a free negro) his mark is under saw tooth the right ear & over saw tooth the left ear
May 8th	Mr Benj^{a} Moseley's mark over saw tooth the right & left ears
24th	Hezekiah Fentriss's mark swallow fork and a nick under & over the right ear
June 14	Henry son of Henry Moore his mark is crop slit & under keel the right ear and crop the left ear
November	Lemuel Fentriss son of John his mark is flower deluce the right ear swallow fork & nick under the left ear
Decemb^{r} 8	John son of John Wilbur his mark is slit out & nick over the right ear crop & over half crop the left ear
1747 Aprill 1	Mr Adam Thorowgoods mark is crop hole & slit the right ear; and under keel the left ear

Augt 22 Nathaniel Martin his mark is hole in the right ear & under half crop the left ear

Octobr 3 Robert Cartwright his mark is swallow fork the left ear under & over keel the right ear

William Cartwrights mark is under & over keel the right ear crop & slit & a small piece taken out of the upper side of the left ear

William (son of Leml) Cornick his mark is crop the left ear & under half crop the right ear

Novr 13 John Henly (son of John) his mark is crop & under keel the right ear and over keel the left ear

Nath Huggins mark is crop & over keel the right ear & swallow fork the left ear which mark was formerly Wm Weblins & agreed by his brother Geo: that Robert Huggins should record it for the above Nath

Markam Huggins his mark is swallow fork the right ear crop & over keel the left ear

FebEy 3 Mr Samuel Boush his mark is a hole in the right ear & crop & a hole in the left ear

1748 Mar 26 Rachel daughter of John Wilbur her mark is crop & over half crop the left ear slit & under keel the right ear

Matthew Matthias his mark is crop both ears & a hole in the right

Septr 27 Elizabeth Fentriss her mark is crop & a hole the right ear & two slits the under side of left ear

Novembr Thos Wrights mark is crop & hole the right ear under saw tooth & over keel the left ear

Joshua Wrights mark is crop & hole the left ear under saw tooth & over keel the right ear

George Berrys mark is crop & two slitts the right ear & swallow fork the left ear

Page 18

1748

JanEy Charles Gasking his mark is crop & two slitts & under keel the right ear & under keel the left ear

Joshua Gasking mark is crop & slit the right ear the left whole

John son of Thos Cannon his mark is crop & two slitts the right ear slit & under keel the left ear

John Stone junr his mark is swallow fork & under keel the right ear & over keel the left ear

Lemuel Gasking his mark is crop two slitts & under keel the right ear under keel & over slope the left ear

Henry Gasking his mark is crop two slitts & under keel the left ear & under keel the right ear

James Carroway his mark is crop & under slope both ears

Wm Carroway his mark is crop & under slope the right ear crop & slit the left ear

John Cox his mark is crop & a hole the right ear & a hole in the left

William Dyer jun^{r} his mark is swallow fork & under keel both ears

Nathan / son of Eleazar Cherry his mark is over half crop & under keel the right ear & under half crop the left ear

Eleazar Cherry his mark is crop & under & over keel the right ear swallow fork & over keel the left ear the said Cherry agrees if he leaves this county or should die before his daughter in law Marg^{t} Edwards, that then she is to (unreadable) the said mark

Alexander Pooles mark is under keel & over slope the right ear & over slope the left ear

Eliz^{a} Poole daughter of the said Alex^{r} her mark is over slope & under keel the right ear crop two slitts & under keel the left ear

Anthony Burrough his mark is flower deluce the right ear & crop the left ear

Lewis Thelaball's mark is crop & two slits the right ear under over keel & slit the left ear

Charles Nicholson his mark is crop & under half crop the left ear & a hole in the right ear

1749 Henry Harrison / son of Ja^{s} Harrison / his mark is crop & under slope the right ear the left ear whole

Rachel Harrison her mark is crop & under slop the left ear the right ear whole

James Harrison's mark is crop & slit the right ear the left ear whole

Joel son of Joel Cornick his mark is crop the left & over half crop the right ear

Ambross Burfoot mark is under saw tooth the right ear crop slit & under keel the left ear

Henry son of Richd Simmons his mark is swallow fork & under keel the right ear crop & hole the left ear

James Simmons son of ditto his mark is swallow fork & under keel the right ear crop and over saw tooth the left ear

Mrs Sarah Condons mark is crop under keel & slit the right ear crop & under keel the left ear

May 15 Zias Barns his mark is crop & under keel both ears

Michael Eaton his mark is crop under & over keel & a hole in the right ear crop under & over keel the left ear

Thos Ward jun^{r} his mark is flower deluce the right ear crop & under half crop the left ear

Wm Benson his mark is crop & two swallow forks either ear & under keel the contrary ear

John Brown son of Edwd his mark is crop the right ear crop & two slitts the left ear

Isahiah Brown son of d^{o} his mark is crop & two slitts the right ear & crop the left ear

Henry Barns son of John dec^{d} his mark is crop & under keel both ears

Thos Scopers his mark is crop & under keel the right ear & hole the left ear

July Lancaster Lovett / son of Jno / his mark is crop & slit the right ear & flower deluce the left ear

Charles Whitehurst his mark is crop slitt & over keel the right ear the left ear whole

William Shepard / son of Smith / his mark is swallow fork & under keel the right ear and over keel the left ear

Page 19

1749 Augt 12 John Cornick son of Lem^{l} his mark is crop & slitt the left ear over half crop & under keel the right ear

Thos Whitehurst mark crop the right crop & over keel the left ear

James Henly / son of Cornelius / his mark is crop & under saw tooth the right ear under keel & slit the left ear

30th Elizabeth Shepard her mark is swallow fork & under keel the right ear & under half crop the left ear

Septemb^{r} 18 William Dales mark is swallow fork & under keel either ear the other whole

Hillary son of Henry Brinson jun^{r} his mark is swallow fork the right ear crop & under keel the left ear

Dinah Williamson her mark is crop the right ear crop & under slope the left ear

28 Renatus Land son of Edwd his mark is over keel the right ear crop & over keel the left ear

Jeremiah Land son of d^{o} his mark is crop slit & over keel the right ear & over keel the left ear

Henry Brinson son of Rich^{d} his mark is crop slitt & under keel the right ear slit out and over keel the left ear

Rubin Lovett his mark is slit out & nick under the right ear under half crop & two slitts in the short part of the crop in the left ear

Anna Cox her mark is crop & slit the right ear slit out & flower deluce the left ear

Henry Lamounts mark is swallow fork the right & left ears

William Moseley his mark is crop slit & under keel the right ear crop & slit the left ear

Lem^{l} Malbones mark is crop the right ear & a hole in the left ear

Elizabeth Wilbur her mark is slit out the right ear crop over half crop & under keel the left ear

Wm Marriner his mark is crop & over keel the right ear & a hole in the left ear

John Ward's mark is crop & flower deluce the right ear the left ear whole

John Biddle his mark is two slits in each ear

John Dyer his mark is swallow the right ear swallow fork under keel & over keel the left ear

Doctor Christopher Wrights mark is crop the right ear & over slope the left ear

Argall Thorowgood son of Mr John Thorowgood Senr his mark is a hole in the right ear & under keel the left ear

Doct Robt Paterson's mark is swallow fork & under keel the right ear & crop & under half crop the left ear

Jonathan Fentriss son of Jno his mark is under half crop the right ear swallow fork & under keel the left ear

Mr William Malbones mark is over slope & under keel the left ear

Idem's mark is over slop & under nick the right ear which mark was his grandfathers

James Williamson his mark is swallow fork the right ear & under saw tooth the left ear

1750 John Thorowgood Keeling his mark is crop the right ear & over slope the left

May 5 William Mays mark is swallow fork the right ear crop slitt & under keel the left ear

Thos Owens his mark is a hole in the right ear crop & slit the left ear

Patrick Brooks his mark is crop both ears & a hole in the left ear

Frances Morris his mark is under half crop the right ear & flower deluce the left ear

Adam Lovetts mark is crop & two slitts the right ear flower deluce & slit out the left ear

Wm Gaskings his mark is crop & two slitts the left ear the right ear whole

Mary Gaskings her mark is crop & two slitts the left ear flower deluce & slit out the right

Edward Cannons mark is crop & slit the right ear crop & over slit the left ear

Wm / son of Wm Wilbur his mark is crop & over half crop the left ear under saw tooth the right ear

Richd Simmons his mark is crop the left ear & slit the right ear

1750 Augt 18 John Matthias son of Henry his mark is crop & slit the left ear cut in the under side of the right ear & cut square out down to the root thereof

John Lovett son of Lancaster his mark is crop & two slitts the right ear & flower deluce the left ear

Anna Burgess daughter of Henry her mark is crop & slit the right ear & a hole in the left ear

Henry Burgess his mark is swallow fork under & over keel the right ear under keel the left ear

Simon Snaile son of Henry his mark is crop & under half crop the right ear & slit out the left ear

Thos Finkley's mark is crop & under nick either ear

John Atwoods mark is crop & under keel the right ear & slit out the left ear

Thos Atwoods mark is slit out the right ear crop & under keel the left ear

Abell Edmonds his mark is swallow fork & under nick the right the left hole

Wm son of Wm Cornick his mark is crop & two slits the right ear & over half crop the left ear

Mary daughter of Wm Brinson her mark is swallow fork the left ear & nick under the right ear

Anthony Whitehurst (son of Robt) his mark is swallow fork & under keel both ears

Francis Shepard wido her mark is swallow fork & under keel the right ear & over keel the left ear

William Carrel senr his mark is crop under keel & a hole in the right & left ears

John Scopers his mark is a hole in the right ear & crop the left

1751 Aprill 23rd Charles Webb his mark is a hole in the right ear & crop the left

Jacob son of Adam Keeling his mark is crop & flower deluce the left & a hole in the right

Lemuel Cartwright his mark is crop & under keel the right ear & a hole in the left ear

Benjamin Ward / son of Jno decd / his mark is crop & flower deluce the right ear

John Ward / son of do / his mark is swallow fork the right ear & under saw tooth the left ear

June Margt Wilbur her mark is crop & over half crop the left ear & slit out the right ear

Octobr 11 Elizabeth Smyth / daughter of Tully Robinson Smyth / her mark is crop slit under & over keel the right ear crop slit & under keel the left ear

Tully Robinson Smyth his mark is swallow fork the right ear & over saw tooth the left ear which mark was his fathers

Anthony Lawsons mark is crop the right ear & slit out the left

Adam Gornor son of Rich^{d} dec^{d} / his mark is crop the right & nick und^{r} the left ear

November 14 Anne Robinson daughter of Mr William Robinson her mark is under keel the right & left ears

Thurman Hoggard his mark is a slit & over keel the right ear crop & under keel the left ear

Anthy Moseley son of Capt Anthy Moseley his mark is under keel the right & over keel the left

Andrew Stewart his mark is crop & under keel the right ear crop under & over keel the left ear

William Robinson / son of Adam / his mark is swallow fork & under keel the right ear crop half crop & slit the left ear

John Bonney (son of Edwd) swallow fork & flower deluce either ear the other whole

James Williamsons mark is under keel & slit the right ear & under keel the left ear

Argall Thorowgoods mark is swallow fork the right ear & under saw tooth the left

John Bonney Senr his mark is crop slit & under keel the right & left ears

Jonathan son of ditto his mark is crop & over keel the right ear over slope the left

Nathan son of ditto his mark is crop & two slitts the right ear the left whole

John son of ditto his mark is crop slit & under keel the left ear & under half (faded)

Henry Small his mark is under & over keel the right ear the left whole

Mr John Jnu? jun^{r} his mark is crop & under half crop the right & left (faded)

Drew Whitehurst son of Batson his mark is swallow fork the right ear & over keel the (faded)

William Fentriss his mark is crop the right ear & under slope the left ear

John son of George Weblin / is under keel the right ear crop under keel & slit the (faded)

Anthony McKeels mark is crop & hole the right ear

Benjamin Dingly Gray his mark is crop & over half crop both ears

1761 Charles Killey's mark is hole and crop in the right ear and under saw tooth the left

Sarah Killey's mark crop and hole the right ear & crop and under saw tooth the left ear

Jo(torn) Thorowgood's mark is swallow fork either ear

(torn) mark is swallow fork both ears & slit either ear

Written on separate slips of paper

This ___ Mr George Hancocke of
Princess Anne County Gent ___ heirs ___
& administrator to pay or ___ be paid
unto Mr ChristopE Cocke the ___ or order
in the full & just sum of thirty one __
fourteen ____ ___ _____

____ _____ ____ __
On demand ___ ____ ____ ____
_____ my hand
this day of May anno 1696

The 24th day of June 1712
ME Captin Cocke sir o_? desier
you to record a near _? for my
brother James Leggit the mark
is cropt and under ceale of the
left ear and slot of the right
and so doing you will obblege
your frind and servant to
command david Leggit
and sir o_? desier you to send a
coppe of it by the carer herreof

Index

A

B

C

D

E

F

G

H

I

J

K

L

M

N

O

P

R

S

Books by Michael Schoettle

- Princess Anne County Virginia List of Earmarks and Brands, 1691 – 1778 (2015)
- Abstracts of Princess Anne County Virginia Deed Book 1, 1691 – 1708 (2015)
- Abstracts of Princess Anne County Virginia Deed Book 2, 1708 – 1714 (2015)
- Princess Anne County Virginia Order Book No. 1, 1691 – 1709 (2015)

These books may be purchased directly from the author by contacting him at pacgenealogy@gmail.com.

He may also be contacted by writing to:

Michael Schoettle
17041 Thousand Oaks Dr
Haymarket, VA 20169

www.ingramcontent.com/pod-product-compliance
Lightning Source LLC
Chambersburg PA
CBHW080405270326
41927CB00015B/3355